KT-465-140

# Mastering Spreadsheet Budgets and Forecasts

## How to save time and gain control of your business

■ ■ ■

## MALCOLM SECRETT

the Institute of Management

FOUNDATION

PITMAN PUBLISHING

London · Hong Kong · Johannesburg
Melbourne · Singapore · Washington DC

The Institute of Management (IM) is at the
forefront of management development and
best management practice. The Institute
embraces all levels of management from
students to chief executives. It provides a
unique portfolio of services for all managers,
enabling them to develop skills and achieve
management excellence.

If you would like to hear more about the
benefits of membership, please write to
Department P, Institute of Management,
Cottingham Road, Corby NN17 1TT.

This series is commissioned by the
Institute of Management Foundation.

PITMAN PUBLISHING
128 Long Acre, London WC2E 9AN
Tel: +44 (0)171 447 2000
Fax: +44 (0)171 240 5771

A Division of Pearson Professional Limited

First published in Great Britain 1993
This edition published in 1997

ISBN 0 273 62684 1

*British Library Cataloguing in Publication Data*
A CIP catalogue record for this book can be obtained from the British Library.

10 9 8 7 6 5 4 3 2 1

Typeset by Northern Phototypesetting Co. Ltd., Bolton
Printed and bound in Great Britain by Bell and Bain Ltd, Glasgow
*The Publishers' policy is to use paper manufactured from sustainable forests.*

# Contents

■ ■ ■

| | | |
|---|---|---|
| **Foreword** | | iv |
| **Introduction** | | ix |

### Part 1: BUDGETING AND FORECASTING ESSENTIALS
**1**

**1 Understanding budgets and forecasts** — 3

Budgets and budget forecasts — 4
Profit and loss forecasts — 6
Cash flow forecasts — 7
Spreadsheet-based budgets and forecasts for
    day-to-day management — 10
Forecasts are not the sole province of accountants — 11

**2 Using budgets and forecasts** — 15

Budget management — 16
Planning and 'What-if' — 17
Cost control — 18
Raising finance — 18
Cash flow control — 20

### Part 2: SPREADSHEET ESSENTIALS
**23**

**3 Understanding computer spreadsheets** — 25

Prelude — 26
What spreadsheets are — 27
Principal facilities and functions, examples of their use — 28
Multi-sheet and three-dimensional spreadsheets — 46

iii

## 4 Spreadsheet techniques for budgeting and forecasting

49

A multitude of ways and means     50

Essential practices and conventions     50

Example forecasts     56

Examples of non-essential, but useful techniques     69

## Part 3: A COMPLETE FORECAST FROM BEGINNING TO END

75

## 5 Preparations for the budget

77

Review of the budgeting process     78

The example business 'Widget Makers Ltd'     79

Deciding the requirements of the example budget     80

A single or departmental budget?     80

Cost categories: definitions and examples     82

Cost headings     88

Categorising the cost headings     91

Revenue headings     93

The forecast's duration and periods     94

## 6 Creating the budget framework

97

The sales forecast     98

The budget forecast     99

The cash flow forecast     103

## Part 4: USING THE FORECAST

115

## 7 Assembling the budget

117

Making the sales forecast     118

Making the budget forecast     120

Cash flow forecast adjustments     128

Graphs and key indicators     132

Key ratios     134

## 8 Causes and effects   139

The reiteration process   140
Practical aspects of examining effects   141
Simple cause and effect   142
Where to start – with the cause or the effect?   147
Gross profitability of each product   166

## 9 Allocation, monitoring and reviewing   171

Budget allocation   172
Simple is best   172
Performance monitoring principles   173
Setting up monitoring for the Widget Makers Ltd forecast   180
Recording actual figures   185
Reviewing the forecast   188

## 10 Further analysis   199

The impact of change on cash flow   200
The effect of rapid growth on cash flow   207
What-if analysis   208

## Part 5: HANDLING VAT   211

## 11 VAT in the forecast   213

What is VAT?   214
Calculating and paying VAT   215
Cash flow forecast VAT calculations   216

**Appendix 1: Computer and spreadsheet glossary**   224
**Appendix 2: Budget and forecasting glossary**   226
**Index**   228

# Foreword

■ ■ ■

## What this book will do for you

Whether you are a line manager in the private or public sector, or a businessman running your own enterprise, this book will lead you step by step, using everyday English, through all of the important principles of budgeting and forecasting, and show you how to construct and use them on a computer spreadsheet.

Whether or not you have ever before prepared a budget or touched a computer keyboard, the objective is that you will be able to build and use budgets and forecasts that are precisely matched to your needs.

You will also be shown how computer-based forecasts are so very much more useful than their pen and paper predecessors.

Questions and aspirations like these are addressed:

> Whether or not you have ever before prepared a budget or touched a computer keyboard, the objective is that you will be able to build and use budgets and forecasts that are precisely matched to your needs.

*'Budgets and forecasts always take so long, can a computer spreadsheet speed things up and make them easier?'*

*'I've heard of computer spreadsheets, they sound as though they may be useful to me, but I'm not really sure.'*

*'The department has been told that all our budgets must be submitted on computer spreadsheets next time, and I've been looking for something to help us learn how to prepare them.'*

*'The bank manager has said the finance will only be made available if a satisfactory operating budget and cash flow are prepared. Maybe a spreadsheet will help?'*

*'Maybe a computer spreadsheet would help us to prepare and evaluate several different business plans very quickly.'*

Now – budgets and forecasts are, by their nature, very dynamic in the literal sense of the word, something never more true than when they are prepared using a computer spreadsheet. Books on the other hand are not, by their nature, dynamic in this literal sense – and there is a great danger that through them one of the most important and interesting tools available to managers is perceived as a dry and dusty subject.

So, there is clearly a requirement to convey an understanding of budgets and forecasts in a way that does not send the reader into a deep slumber, despite their best intentions. And, equally importantly, to do so in a way that clearly shows what practical and dynamic day-to-day management tools they can be when computer spreadsheets are applied to the task.

I have endeavoured to address these needs in three ways:

*Firstly* – by eliminating accountancy and computer jargon wherever possible. Where the use of technical terms is unavoidable they are explained in the text, usually when they first occur. There is also a full glossary of terms.

*Secondly* – by using straightforward and relevant examples and illustrations from settings familiar to any manager or businessman.

*Thirdly* – by making a computer disc available to readers that contains the actual spreadsheet models used in the book. The idea here is, partly to provide an opportunity for obtaining hands-on experience using spreadsheets for budgeting, and partly as additional emphasis to aid and accelerate understanding.

Budgets and forecasts are viewed by managers and businessmen in many different ways, for example:

- Allocating and controlling expenditure.

- Forecasting and monitoring sales volumes and revenue.

- Departmental breakdown of the whole company's budget.

- Supporting information for a business plan.

- The basis of a bid for raising finance, or obtaining higher level authority for a revised strategy.

- Profit and loss forecasting.

- Cash flow forecasting.

There is no 'right' or 'wrong' use of budgets and forecasts. Although the list probably covers their most common uses, in reality there are as many applications as there are managers.

However, there has been a revolution in budgets and forecasts since computers became an essential piece of office equipment. Before computers, budgets and forecasts were very lengthy and tedious processes, and thus necessarily only carried out or reviewed at infrequent intervals of a year or more. Because of these scarce reviews, and because real world circumstances can change significantly in very much shorter periods, prac-

Budgets and forecasts can now be prepared in hours and reviewed in minutes. They can be used to test 'What if' scenarios, combine several departmental budgets into one, and provide accurate cash flow forecasts.

tically minded managers, quite rightly, paid little heed to these forecasts. They certainly only ever used them for day-to-day decision making with a good deal of care and caution.

Computers have changed all this. Budgets and forecasts can now be prepared in hours and reviewed in minutes. They can be used to test 'What-if' scenarios, combine several departmental budgets into one, and provide accurate cash flow forecasts. In short, computer spreadsheet based forecasts have become one of the most powerful and essential operational tools available to managers of all disciplines.

If you have previously prepared budgets on paper, you will certainly appreciate the enormous advantages of using a spreadsheet, and quickly see how very much more you will be able to do with them. And all of those things you had wished were either possible or practicable, you will now find can be easily realised.

Finally, I earnestly hope you will find the book interesting, beneficial, and most of all – enjoyable.

*Malcolm Secrett*
*Ilkley, West Yorkshire.*

# Introduction

■ ■ ■

## The structure of the book

There are five main parts, dealing with:

> Part 1 – Budgeting and forecasting essentials.
>
> Part 2 – Spreadsheet essentials.
>
> Part 3 – A complete forecast from beginning to end.
>
> Part 4 – Using the forecast.
>
> Part 5 – Handling VAT.

The book can be read from start to finish, in order, as a complete programme. Alternatively or subsequently, individual parts can be selected and read in isolation, or dipped into by way of reference. The Contents provide a summary of topics to help find the section required; for a more detailed search, the Index has a comprehensive list of key words and subjects.

> **The book can be read from start to finish, in order, as a complete programme. Alternatively or subsequently, individual parts can be selected and read in isolation, or dipped into by way of reference.**

Accountancy, computer and other jargon has been kept to a minimum, nevertheless its use is essential in places. All specialised words and phrases are explained either within the text or one of the appended glossaries.

## Reference to computer spreadsheet

Because of the dynamic nature of budgets and forecasts applied to spreadsheets, and because spreadsheets themselves are inherently so versatile and dynamic in their own right, your understanding of both will be considerably enhanced and accelerated if you use a spreadsheet in conjunction with the book. You will undoubtedly want to try out some of the examples and illustrations on your spreadsheet, and the book has therefore been designed with this specifically in mind.

You can either construct the examples for yourself, or obtain a copy of the illustration disc which has all of them ready for immediate use, complete with graphs and charts.

Throughout the book you will see these symbols:

> ★ means looking at a spreadsheet on a computer will be helpful.
> **★EXnn** means use of the specific example on a spreadsheet will be helpful, whether you have constructed it yourself, or use the ready made version on the illustrated disc.

If you intend to build the examples yourself, or use the ready-made models on the illustration disc, you will in either case need a spreadsheet program on your computer. Part 2 explains what you will need to know about spreadsheets.

## The illustration disc

The illustration disc is optional – the book is complete in itself and may be used throughout without any reference to a computer, but comprehension will be significantly improved if a spreadsheet is used to try the various examples.

The disc contains ready-made versions of all of the examples used in the book. It can be supplied in Microsoft Excel or Lotus 1-2-3 format on a 3½" disc.

The purchaser of the illustration disc will be registered, and entitled to telephone guidance and assistance in the use of the models.

To obtain a copy of the illustration disc, simply send a cheque or postal order for £12.00, made payable to MALCOLM SECRETT, to:

Malcolm Secrett
PO Box 51
Ilkley
West Yorkshire
LS29 0XX

**Important** – Please state:
1   Spreadsheet type and version number. (The version number will be shown on the master disc supplied with the spreadsheet, and on the screen when the spreadsheet is loaded.)
2   Your name, address and telephone number.

Within a few days you will receive your disc and registration details.

# PART 1

■ ■ ■

# Budgeting and forecasting essentials

This first part of the book establishes the context and boundaries of budgeting and forecasting, as they are addressed and illustrated, using computer spreadsheets.

It deals with what budgets and forecasts are, and how they can be used.

It is sometimes supposed that certain aspects of budgeting and forecasting dictate that only accountants will have the necessary skills to understand, create and use them. This supposition is unquestionably wrong.

# 1
. . .

# Understanding budgets and forecasts

3

Budgets and budget forecasts ■

Profit and loss forecasts ■

Cash flow forecasts ■

Spreadsheet-based budget and forecasts for day-to-day
management ■

Forecasts are not the sole province of accountants ■

# Budgets and budget forecasts

■ ■ ■

Although the terms *budget* and *budget forecast* are sometimes inter-preted in different ways, the definitions we will use are probably the most widely accepted versions.

If you already have very clear definitions in your mind that don't accord with those in the book, don't worry, it won't matter at all. You will undoubtedly recognise the detailed circumstances being described later on, and the method of handling them will be just as valid. They may just be called by another name.

Here are my definitions:

> *A budget is a statement of **allocated** expenditure and/or revenue, under specific headings, for a chosen period. Generally the expenditure allocation must not be exceeded, and the revenue must be achieved.*

4

> *A budget forecast is a statement of **expected** expenditure and/or revenue, based on the best information to hand, under specific headings, for a chosen period.*

To illustrate these, let's just look at a couple of examples. The first in a company department with a central supporting role, the second in a department close to the sharp end of the business, an operational role. In both cases the 'department' may consist of any number of staff and managers, including just one person.

## Example 1 – The central role

The wages department, accounts, general administration, purchasing, secretarial pool, public relations can all be considered examples of central support if their function embraces most other departments in the company. We'll consider the wages department.

As part of the company's annual budgeting process, the wages department are asked to prepare an estimate of expenditure over the coming year. They will probably need to think about such things as staff costs, stationery and computer maintenance.

To do this they will prepare a forecast, or expectation, of expenditure against various headings for a given period – usually 12 months. This is a *budget forecast*, which is then submitted as a bid for an allocation of money to cover the expenditure. After due process by the company an allocation of money is made, this is now a *budget*. The department is then expected to operate throughout the year within the constraints of the budget – see Figure 1.1 (below).

**Figure 1.1   Summary of a budget forecast/bid/allocation process**

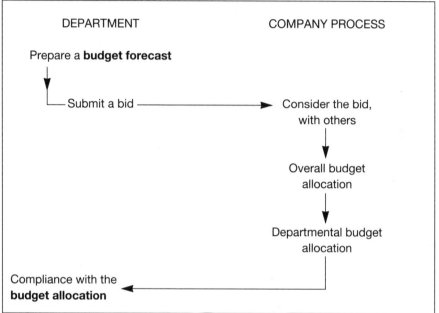

It is less likely in a support department, than in one directly involved with the sharp end of the business, that there will be any need to alter the budget allocation through the year.

## Example 2 – The operational role

The factory, sales team, service staff and distribution can all be considered examples of operational departments, for our purposes, if their work load is directly or closely related to the volume of business. We'll look at the sales team.

They are asked to prepare an estimate of not only expenditure, but also sales revenue, over the coming year for their department. To do this they will prepare a forecast of expenditure and revenue against various headings. Now, whilst it *may* be possible in some circumstances to prepare both expenditure and sales revenue forecasts independently, it is more likely that each will be dependent upon the other in some way.

To take a simple example, if sales performance is partly determined by the number of visits made by travelling salesmen, then the greater the selling effort made, the greater the cost of cars, petrol and overnight accommodation.

Thus the expenditure and revenue forecasts must be prepared in concert, and linked by any factors that will affect both, such as the costs of travelling salesmen, advertising expenditure and so on. This combined revenue and expenditure *budget forecast* is submitted to the company's budgeting process as a bid for the coming year.

In the same way as for the wages department a *budget allocation* is made, but in this case there will be a relationship between revenue and expenditure. Taking our simple example again, the expenditure allocation for travel expenses will be expressed as a proportion of sales revenue, and the sales team will be expected to operate throughout the year so that travel expenditure doesn't exceed the proportion of sales revenue allocated.

Because of the changeable nature of business, there is a very high probability that the budget forecast of operational departments would benefit from review, and amendment if necessary, throughout the year. But so long as the relationships between revenue and any variable costs, such as travelling expenses, have been explicitly stated in the budget allocation, then it will be unnecessary to alter the allocation in the light of a new forecast.

If no such relationship has been included, then whenever sales expectations change throughout the year the budget allocation will also need to be reviewed, and probably amended, after a new forecast.

There are of course other factors to be considered in this area of budgeting, and we'll be looking at these in the next chapter.

# Profit and loss forecasts
■ ■ ■

In accountancy there is a very precise definition for the word *profit*, but we have no need for the absolute detail of its meanings, a general definition will be sufficient for our purpose.

Profit is the difference between *trading revenues and costs*, that is, what is left from the sales revenue after subtracting all expenses. Money spent on capital items – things owned by the company that have a value which could be realised by selling them – are usually excluded from the calculation of profit. However, any reduction in the value of capital items during the year, which is known as depreciation, will normally be considered a trading expense, and hence will figure in the calculation of profit. Profit can be described as 'gross' or 'net':

**gross profit = revenue – direct costs**

**net profit = revenue – (direct costs + overhead costs)**

*Direct costs* are those incurred expressly on the product – raw materials for manufacturing, or spare parts for a maintenance service, for example.

*Overhead costs* are those that are incurred independently of the product, such as rent, rates, general administration, and so on.

Although we will occasionally be referring to gross profit, we will be mainly interested in net profit. In this book, and elsewhere, if the word *profit* is used by itself, it means *net profit*.

Loss is simply a negative value of profit. Here is a definition of a *profit and loss* (P&L) *forecast*:

> *A profit and loss forecast is exactly like a budget forecast, except that only revenues and expenses considered part of the profit calculation are included.*

7

# Cash flow forecasts
■  ■  ■

Whereas budget and P&L forecasts are concerned with expense incurred and revenue earned, *cash flow* refers to the movement of cash in and out of the company or department. And they are by no means the same thing. In our everyday lives we frequently encounter the difference, for instance, a salaried person earns their income throughout a month, but only receives the cash for it once a month. Whenever a credit or charge card is used to buy something, its value is acquired immediately, but the cash to pay for it is only spent when the credit card account is paid.

Business is no different, indeed, one could say that business has a credit culture of very long standing. It is fairly normal to expect at least 30 days' credit from suppliers when buying, and to provide a similar period of credit to business customers on your sales. Thus the cash in and out of the business will be offset from the time that expenses are incurred – buying stationery for instance, and from the time that sales revenues are earned – or, supplying your product or service for instance, by the period of credit allowed (or taken!) for each.

Here is a definition of a cash flow forecast:

> *A cash flow forecast has exactly the same headings as a budget forecast. It shows cash flowing in and out of the business, offset in time from when expenses are incurred, or revenue is earned.*

Thirty days' credit from a supplier can be illustrated like this:

**Figure 1.2  Thirty days' credit from a supplier**

| | Jan | Feb | Mar | Apr | May | Jun | Jul | Aug | Sep | Oct | Nov | Dec |
|---|---|---|---|---|---|---|---|---|---|---|---|---|
| **EXPENSE** Stationery (£) | | 350 | 100 | | 450 | | | | | | | |
| **CASH OUT** STATIONERY (£) | | | 350 | 100 | | 450 | | | | | | |

and credit of 30 days given to customers, like this:

**Figure 1.3  Thirty days' credit for customers**

| | Jan | Feb | Mar | Apr | May | Jun | Jul | Aug | Sep | Oct | Nov | Dec |
|---|---|---|---|---|---|---|---|---|---|---|---|---|
| **REVENUE** Product "A" (£) | | | 400 | | 6500 | | 3750 | | | | | |
| **CASH IN** Product "A" (£) | | | | 4000 | | 6500 | | 3750 | | | | |

Clearly, when in reality there are many items of expense, each with its own period of credit allowed, and perhaps several sales items, again each with its own period of credit given, then the calculation of the net effect on cash flow each month can be quite complicated. Fortunately, it is no problem whatever when using a computer spreadsheet.

# The importance of understanding cash flow

Cash, in the end, is the life blood of any business, and there are many, many things that can affect how much there is in the bank at any one time. In any company there will be few, if any, managers who will not have responsibility for something that can impact on cash flow.

Here is a list of some things that impact *positively* on cash flow. Positive means that cash arrives in the bank earlier, or leaves it later, or isn't spent in the first place.

In all cases listed, the converse of the statement will have a *negative* impact on cash flow. Negative means that cash arrives in the bank later, or leaves it earlier, or is spent unnecessarily – see Table 1.1.

Of course, these must be taken in the context of good and ethical business practice, and maintaining an appropriate level of quality of service or goods.

**Table 1.1   Positive impacts on cash flow**

- Taking full advantage of supplier's credit
- Minimising credit offered to customers
- Minimising credit taken by customers
- Minimising sales invoice preparation delays
- Minimising sales invoice dispatch delays
- Making the best choice between buying/leasing options
- Minimising levels of sales stock
- Minimising levels of raw and manufacturing materials stock
- Minimising material processing times
- Best possible match of production levels to sales
- Minimising the period between manufacture and sale

Now, all of the things listed above are processes, disciplines or policies that will impact positively and directly on cash flow. But the obvious must not be forgotten – the fact that every good business decision will also immediately, or ultimately, impact positively on cash flow. And conversely, a bad decision will have a negative impact.

Before leaving cash flow, we'll just consider how the *type* of business can also influence cash flow by looking at two illustrations, one that is inherently a good business for cash flow, and another that is not.

Starting with the one that is not a good cash business.

### Firework manufacture in the UK

The number of fireworks bought and used around 5 November each year is very much higher than at any other time. But the firework manufacturer will have been making them for this annual explosion for some months before the event. In those preceding months they have to buy materials, manufacture the fireworks, pack them, market them, and finally distribute them – this with all its attendant expenditure and cash drain, without a penny piece coming back into the bank for them until sometime around 5 November.

In this illustration, the most significant factor affecting cash flow is a sales demand level and duration grossly out of proportion to the relatively long and cash demanding manufacturing cycle.

**Note:** The example is slightly contrived, because in reality companies in this business will take measures to reduce the impact.

9

Now an example of a good cash business.

### The supermarket

Supermarkets buy their stock in very large quantities and obtain volume discounts. They receive the normal 30 days' credit before they pay for the stock. The stock is immediately put out on the shelves, to be bought by customers who straight away pay cash for their purchases.

In this example, the most significant factor affecting cash flow is the combination of credit on purchases and immediate cash payment for sales.

An understanding of cash flow is important for managers in many different roles, for even where their responsibilities do not include direct control of cash, it is very probable that the consequences of their decisions and actions will have an impact on it.

# Spreadsheet-based budgets and forecasts for day-to-day management

■ ■ ■

The data contained in budgets, forecasts, and the 'actual' figures collected for comparison, are a potential source of strikingly informative and useful information about the performance of the company. By performance I mean the broadest sense of the word, which certainly includes direct financial management and control, but also such things as staff efficiency, stock control, departmental or product line profitability comparisons, and many, many more.

> An understanding of cash flow is important for managers in many different roles, for even where their responsibilities do not include direct control of cash, it is very probable that the consequences of their decisions and actions will have an impact on it.

There is nothing new in the awareness of this potential, but in the past it has been exceedingly difficult and time consuming to unlock it. Managers have been frustrated by the knowledge that so much useful information, which would be so helpful both strategically and in their day-to-day decision making, could only be extracted by lengthy and painstaking work with pen and paper. To be sure, the process was eased by the advent of office calculating machines, but even then a budget forecast rework to reflect changing circumstances, or to examine a proposed new strategy, could take literally days and produce only very basic information for decision taking.

For instance, try to imagine the combination of calculations that would be necessary if, in the coming year, all of the following were taken into account in the forecast of a company manufacturing 20 product lines:

■ overall sales growth for the year of 12 per cent;

■ overlaid seasonal sales fluctuations of 15 per cent during the second quarter, and 25 per cent during the fourth quarter;

■ price increases of 7 per cent for 63 per cent of the raw materials for 13 of the product lines;

■ production line efficiency improvement of 3 per cent;

■ wages and salary increases of 5 per cent from the eighth month onwards.

Enough is enough! That was only scratching the surface of just one requirement from budget forecasts. And what about collecting real figures to compare with the forecast, and then to reforecast based on the trends thus established, and take into account whatever changes in circumstances have occurred since the forecast was first made? Clearly it isn't the sort of thing we would be able to do with pen and paper more than once a year at the most, or maybe not at all.

Now the use of computer spreadsheets has revolutionised budgeting and forecasting, they have relegated to the past the frustration of inaccessible information. All of the things that were difficult or just totally impracticable with pen and paper can now be taken for granted, and carried out in hours and minutes. Forecasts, which were once a tedious annual chore, to be quickly consigned to a filing cabinet, never to see the light of day again, are now a dynamic and day-to-day operational tool for all managers.

By not forecasting, by not testing strategic alternatives, and by not monitoring achievement, we are not in full control of our business. The competitive world we are in gives very little leeway for anything less than full control, or anything less than maximum efficiency from the personnel and material resources at our disposal.

# Forecasts are not the sole province of accountants
■ ■ ■

It is sometimes supposed that certain aspects of budgeting and forecasting dictate that only accountants will have the necessary skills to understand, create and use them. This supposition is unquestionably wrong. Whilst accountancy skills are a valuable asset for any company in many ways, they are not required for budgeting and forecasting. Indeed, it can be argued, as it is by me, that the most important contribution to bud-

> If, nevertheless, your company's policy is that only the accountant's department will prepare budget forecasts and allocations, they will undoubtedly appreciate your understanding of what they are trying to achieve, and you will more readily understand the process by which they have arrived at the outcome.

geting and forecasting is a clear understanding of the day-to-day operation of that part of the business for which we are responsible.

The additional requirements are nothing more than an understanding of very simple arithmetic, and an appreciation of how essential to our own management control budgets and forecasts are. The first of these I will take for granted, the second you will either already have, or will do so, I'm sure, by the time we have finished.

If, nevertheless, your company's policy is that only the accountant's department will prepare budget forecasts and allocations, they will undoubtedly appreciate your understanding of what they are trying to achieve, and you will more readily understand the process by which they have arrived at the outcome. Thus you will be able to make a more significant input to your budget, and ensure that your requirements have been properly understood and incorporated.

## Summary

In this chapter we have:

- Agreed definitions for *budget* and *budget forecast*.
- Outlined the basic process of budget forecasting, submission of a bid and budget allocation.
- Agreed definitions for *profit and loss* and *cash flow* forecasts.

We have also seen:

- the similarities and differences in the process between central supporting and operational departments;
- that sales revenue and related variable costs can be linked in both the forecast and the allocation;
- why spreadsheets have made budgets and forecasts such useful tools for management control and decision making;
- that the most significant input to budgets and forecasts is a clear understanding of day-to-day operations.

13

There is nothing whatever wrong with gut feelings, on the contrary, managers' experience and expertise in the business is the driving force behind their instincts, and it would be foolhardly indeed to ignore them. But, and it is a big but, when instinct alone is applied to complex situations that can easily be reduced to objective measurement, then the perpetrators have no one but themselves to blame for the consequences.

# 2
■ ■ ■

# Using budgets and forecasts

15

Budget management ■

Planning and 'What-if' ■

Cost control ■

Raising finance ■

Cash flow control ■

**O**ur perception of how budgets and forecasts are used, if we have any view at all, will be based principally upon our own experience, and knowledge of our company's policies. In practice though, so flexible are budgets and forecasts, there can be as many variants of their application as there are individual managers. Again I reiterate that none of the variants are 'wrong', they have just been created to fulfil the special requirements of a particular circumstance.

So whilst we look at these common and fundamental classes of application, please bear in mind that there can be any number of variations on the basic themes.

# Budget management

■ ■ ■

In Chapter 1 we looked at an outline of basic budgets and forecasts, and saw how the process of forecasting can lead to a budget allocation. The objectives of making a budget allocation will usually include:

- setting maximum limits on expenditure;
- setting minimum limits on revenue where appropriate;
- ensuring a common awareness of the limits;
- providing a basis for performance monitoring;
- highlighting the level of costs, one with another.

Because most expenditure occurs at intervals, usually monthly or quarterly, throughout the budget period, it is better to present the allocation for each heading in calendarised form, using the shortest interval that occurs between successive payments, such as monthly or four weekly (budget periods and span are dealt with in more detail in Chapter 5).

Thus, if a one-year allocation for stationery is £24,000, and it is expected that the costs will be incurred evenly throughout the year, then it is simply shown as a monthly cost of £2,000.

Electricity for the office on the other hand will be billed quarterly, in say February, May, August and November. The annual total is £3,500, but because of seasonal fluctuations, each quarter's bill will be different.

These two items of expenditure can therefore be presented thus:

**Figure 2.1  Presentation of expenditure**

| Item | Jan | Feb | Mar | Apr | May | Jun | Jul | Aug | Sep | Oct | Nov | Dec | Total |
|---|---|---|---|---|---|---|---|---|---|---|---|---|---|
| Stationery | 2000 | 2000 | 2000 | 2000 | 2000 | 2000 | 2000 | 2000 | 2000 | 2000 | 2000 | 2000 | 24000 |
| Electricity | | 1250 | | | 1000 | | | 500 | | | 750 | | 3500 |
| Monthly totals | 2000 | 3250 | 2000 | 2000 | 3000 | 2000 | 2000 | 2500 | 2000 | 2000 | 2750 | 2000 | 27500 |

This simple layout already provides quite a bit of information:

- annual total for each item of expenditure;
- monthly amount for each item of expenditure;
- monthly total expenditure;
- annual total expenditure.

It enables all of the objectives to be met. Limits by item and month are clearly shown – everyone can see them so there is a common awareness. The calendarisation enables performance monitoring month by month, and the level of cost between each item is shown month by month and as an annual total.

In Chapter 9 the method of using 'actual' figures and comparing them with the forecast will be covered.

# Planning and 'What-if'
■ ■ ■

Whenever a budget forecast is created it inevitably begs many questions, such as 'What if the sales of this product were increased by another 2 per cent?', or 'I wonder if that product line is doing much for profits, what if we ceased it?', or 'What if we could reduce distribution costs by 4 per cent?'.

Clearly, if a new forecast were prepared in which any or all of the 'What-if' values were substituted for the originals, then the questions could be answered. And of course this is the way in which *business planning* and *profitability assessment* can be carried out. Instead of waiting until the next forecast is required for a budget allocation bid, a special forecast is prepared explicitly for the purpose of examining 'What-if' scenarios.

Now, many a business has suffered at the hands of 'gut feeling' rather than objective measurement. There is nothing whatever wrong with gut feelings, on the contrary, managers' experience and expertise in the business is the driving force behind their instincts, and it would be foolhardy indeed to ignore them. But, and its a big but, when instinct alone is applied to complex situations that can easily be reduced to objective measurement, then the perpetrators have no one but themselves to blame for the consequences. To be sure, gut feelings will often be at the root of some particular idea which is then tested with a forecast, and sometimes instinct will turn out to be absolutely spot on, but at least if the idea is tested there is objective evidence supporting it.

So, business planning supported by forecasts can be used to address simple changes – such as increasing or decreasing sale volumes, ceasing or starting a new product line, or perhaps taking on additional members of staff. Or equally, it can be used to test strategic proposals, affecting whole departments, or indeed the entire company. And of course, there is no better way of checking the financial viability of ideas for completely new business ventures.

# Cost control

■ ■ ■

The overall impact on profitability of changes to even just one variable cost is by no means obvious until it has been tested in a forecast. Gut feelings are notoriously inaccurate in this area. Managers get hooked on to one particular cost that they 'are absolutely certain' will, if reduced by 5 per cent, make say 10 per cent difference to profitability – only to find that when objective calculations are carried out, the reality is perhaps only a 2 per cent increase to profits.

By properly linking and structuring the costs in a forecast, the consequences of individual and multiple changes can be easily examined to see which combination produces the most effective result, and the sensitivity of each cost can be tested to measure the effect of changes to them on profitability.

An understanding of the effect on profitability of each of the costs provides a properly structured 'priority list' for controlling and, if possible, reducing them. There is an objective measurement for which cost will provide the best return for any time and money spent on it.

# Raising finance

■ ■ ■

Banks and other sources of finance like to lend money, that is the business they are in. But their profit is made from the interest paid to them by the borrower, so clearly, before they agree to lend, they will want to be as sure as they can of the borrower's ability to pay the interest, and of course repay the original sum.

If a department or subsidiary of a large organisation is proposing expansion, the role of 'lender' may be taken by the Board of Directors, or the parent company. The case presented to them will be very similar to that needed for a new business, except that rather than

> *Profitability* can be shown with a profit and loss forecast. Many new ventures or expansion schemes will not be profitable immediately, it may be a year or more before they are sufficiently established to become profitable and repay any initial investment.

receiving interest payments on their investment, they will be direct beneficiaries of a profitable outcome from the proposal.

How is a potential borrower, either looking for finance to start up a new business, or to expand an existing one, to convince a lender that they are a sound investment, that they will be able to pay the interest on the money they want to borrow, or provide an adequate profit for the company as a whole?

There are a great many factors to consider, a potential lender will want to know about such things as:

- Is the product or service likely to sell?
- Are the management team competent in this area?
- What market research has been carried out?
- How profitable will the business be?
- How long will it take to achieve optimum profitability?
- Will the cash flow of the business be acceptable?
- Is the amount of borrowing sought too little, or too much?

How these, and many other relevant factors, should be presented to a potential source of finance is a major topic in its own right, and full discussion of it is neither appropriate nor necessary here, but let's just consider how budgets and forecasts can be used to support a case for additional finance.

*Profitability* can be shown with a profit and loss forecast. Many new ventures or expansion schemes will not be profitable immediately, it may be a year or more before they are sufficiently established to become profitable and repay any initial investment. A profit and loss forecast will inherently show 'break even' – the level of sales that generates sufficient gross profit to cover overheads.

A profit and loss forecast should be prepared that extends to the point in time when a net profit is achieved. It is useful when seeking financial backing to present three versions of the forecast:

1 The maximum sales and minimum expenses that might reasonably be achieved. This can be used as an expression of full potential, perhaps as a target to strive for.

2 The minimum sales and maximum expenses expected in the worst case. This determines the maximum financial support that will be required.

3 The most realistic and likely level of sales and expenditure. This will be the enduring operational forecast, the one that will be used for budget allocations and against which performance will be monitored.

*Cash flow forecasts* are an absolutely essential part of the case where finance is being sought from sources external to the company, for instance from a bank. They will also be required by internal backers if the cash required is significant compared to the whole company's cash assets.

The cash flow forecast will be directly linked to the profit and loss forecast, and will show the cash demands for each of the three versions. In particular, the second version should be used as the basis for an agreement on the maximum cash that may be required for short periods during the overall duration of the forecast.

20

# Cash flow control
■  ■  ■

We have just seen how a cash flow forecast can be used to determine cash requirements as part of the supporting information in a bid for finance. Exactly the same principle is used for monitoring and controlling cash flow in the ongoing day-to-day operation of the business or department.

> The cash flow forecast will be directly linked to the profit and loss forecast, and will show the cash demands for each of the three versions.

A cash flow forecast linked to the budget forecast shows how much cash flows in and out of the business each period, and hence the cash balance at the end of each period. Now, whilst some of the factors affecting the balance are unalterable – such as wages, salaries and commitments to our suppliers – other items can be influenced to a greater or lesser degree.

For example, for *cash out* of control, expenditure on building redecoration and other non-trading items can be planned for a month when there will be sufficient, or more, cash available.

The 'just in time' principle for stocks of raw materials and finished goods can be considered. Excessive stock levels are a very common cause of poor cash flow, ideally no more stock than is necessary for requirements should be held ('just in time', or 'JIT', is another subject well worth studying in its own right).

We can also ensure that *cash in* is maximised. Factors that affect it include such things as sales invoice generation and dispatch delays, and late payment by customers.

A cash flow forecast clearly shows the impact each factor will have. Whilst it is easy to imagine the effect of one or two factors without a spreadsheet based forecast, in real life there are always many factors operating in concert, and properly understanding the net effect of all of them certainly defeats my mental capacity. A computer spreadsheet on the other hand is ideally suited to these sort of complexities, and can easily give us a clear view of the whole cash flow picture.

The illustrations we will be looking at later, with the help of a spreadsheet, will confirm and consolidate our understanding of the importance of cash flow forecasts.

## Summary

In this chapter we have seen some of the more common applications for budgets and forecasts:

- *budget allocations* provide high visibility and a sound basis for monitoring and control of expenditure and revenue;

- *budget forecasts* are the foundation of a budget allocation, and are invaluable for business planning, profitability assessment, and 'What-if' testing. They provide for cost control, and are an essential part of the supporting information for raising finance;

- *cash flow forecasts* are also a very important element in a case for additional finance, and most importantly, enable efficient use of a company's cash resources.

# PART 2

. . .

# Spreadsheet essentials

If you have never used a spreadsheet before, and now have access to one, I recommend spending an hour or two on its tutorial program, if it has one. If there isn't an 'on disc' tutorial, learning some basics from the manual and trying out suggestions in this book will provide useful practice and experience.

# 3
. . .

# Understanding computer spreadsheets

Prelude ■

What spreadsheets are ■

Principal facilities and functions, examples of their use ■

Multi-sheet and three-dimensional spreadsheets ■

# Prelude

■ ■ ■

This part of the book will introduce the opportunity to use a computer spreadsheet to aid learning and understanding. There will be two kinds of reference to spreadsheets, they are marked in the left margin, and beside illustration headings with either ★ alone, or with an example or file name after it, for example ★**EX31**. These suggest:

> ★ use of a blank spreadsheet to see or try what is in the text;
> ★**EX31** use of the illustration disc model indicated, or one similar that you have constructed yourself.

The essential functions that are common to all makes of spreadsheet will be demonstrated. Now whilst the way in which these are invoked on different spreadsheets is usually very similar, and sometimes identical, there are nevertheless sufficient differences of detail between the various makes to render a keystroke-by-keystroke account of how to use them impractical.

The illustration disc is supplied in either Excel or Lotus 1-2-3 for Windows or format, as these are currently the two most commonly used spreadsheets in the UK. Other types of spreadsheet from leading manufacturers will also accept one or the other of these formats.

If you have never used a spreadsheet before, and now have access to one, I recommend spending an hour or two on its tutorial program, if it has one. If there isn't an 'on disc' tutorial, learning some basics from the manual and trying out the suggestions in this book will provide useful practice and experience.

> *Tip: Don't try to read a spreadsheet manual like a novel, from beginning to end. Instead, learn a bit, try a bit, learn a bit more, try something slightly more complex, and so on. There is, however, one piece of advice that is applicable to all computer programs: READ THE SCREEN.*

Yes, it is obvious isn't it? But its amazing how quickly we forget the obvious when presented with a new screen. We look, but don't *see and read it*. More often than not, especially on modern software, somewhere on the screen you are told what your options are, or how to put them on the screen.

If you don't have access to a computer and spreadsheet, there is sufficient information in this part of the book to enable you to understand what follows quite satisfactorily.

# What spreadsheets are
■ ■ ■

Spreadsheets on a computer are closely analogous to a simple principle that can be easily explained with pencil and paper.

Let's take a few columns of figures, with totals at the bottom of each one – see Figure 3.1 (below).

**Figure 3.1**

|         |     |     |     |
|---------|-----|-----|-----|
|         | 16  | 12  | 125 |
|         | 4   | 36  | 3   |
|         | 273 | 200 | 46  |
| TOTALS  | 293 | 248 | 174 |

So, for example, the table shows that 293 = 16 + 4 + 273.

Now put some labels on each of the rows and columns, so that each intersection of a column and row can be given a unique identity – see Figure 3.2 (below).

The spaces at the points of intersection of the rows and columns are called *cells*.

**Figure 3.2**

|   | A      | B   | C   | D   |
|---|--------|-----|-----|-----|
| 1 |        | 16  | 12  | 125 |
| 2 |        | 4   | 36  | 3   |
| 3 |        | 273 | 200 | 46  |
| 4 |        |     |     |     |
| 5 | TOTALS | 293 | 248 | 174 |

For example, the number '4' is in cell B2. This description of a cell's position is called its *address*.

Similarly the numbers '16' and '273' are in cells B1 and B3 respectively, and the sum of them all, '293', is in cell B5.

Now, if the figures are replaced with their cell names, the sum can be expressed as in Figure 3.3.

**Figure 3.3**

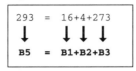

And this is precisely and simply how a spreadsheet works. Figures can be placed in the cells, in exactly the same way as in the paper example. The big difference is that wherever a calculation is needed, the spreadsheet will automatically carry it out when it is entered in (typed into) the cell where the answer is required.

For example, in Figure 3.3, if the calculation 'B1 + B2 + B3' is entered in cell B5 of a spreadsheet, the result '293' will appear in cell B5.

And what's more, if the figure in any cell referred to by cell B5 is changed, say replace the '4' in cell B2 with '50', the new result '339' would immediately appear in cell B5.

Example 3.1 (opposite), is a 'photograph' of Excel on a computer screen. You can see the columns and row border labels, and a replica of the table. The bold rectangle on cell B5 is the 'cursor' – more of this later. But, I have placed it here so that you can see the contents of the cell. It appears near the top of the screen as B1 + B2 + B3. It is the calculation that is giving the result 293.

The position of the cursor can also be seen in another way.

At the top left of the screen is B5, this is also the cursor's position.

OK – so what's all the fuss about if that's all a spreadsheet can do? Well of course, they will do very much more, but the principles are exactly the same throughout – figures, or calculations (formulae) expressed in terms of cell addresses, or both, can be entered in any cell. The results of formulae will always properly reflect any changes made in cells referred to by them.

# Principal facilities and functions: examples of their use
■ ■ ■

This section summarises the most significant functions and capabilities of spreadsheets. Most of them are used in Chapter 4 in the course of building practical example applications.

The subjects covered here are:

- spreadsheet size;
- the cursor, and moving around the spreadsheet;
- entering numbers and text;

## Example 3.1 (∗EX31)

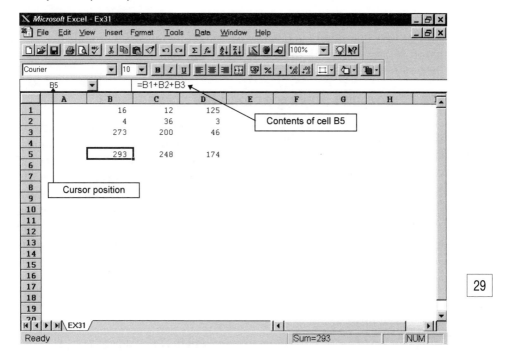

- column width;
- basic arithmetic;
- copying cell contents;
- functions;
- copying a function;
- absolute addresses;
- copying absolute addresses;
- inserting and deleting rows and columns;
- formatting the presentation;
- graphs (charts);
- ranges;
- naming ranges;
- macros;
- printing.

★ Use a spreadsheet to look at and try these functions and facilities.

## Spreadsheet size

Excel has 256 columns and 16,384 rows available. This is far, far more than you are ever likely to need, your budget layout will probably use only 200 to 300 rows, and 15 to 20 columns.

## The cursor, and moving around the spreadsheet

The cursor has two purposes, firstly to enable selection of a cell to make changes to it, and secondly as a 'pointer' to move around the spreadsheet with. Normally only about 20 to 30 rows and 8 to 12 columns can be seen on the screen at any one time, but scrolling up and down, or left and right, reveals any other part of the spreadsheet that is wanted.

The cursor has two purposes, firstly to enable selection of a cell to make changes to it, and secondly as a 'pointer' to move around the spreadsheet with.

The cursor can be moved in a number of ways:

30

★ using the keyboard 'arrow' keys ↑ ↓ → ← to move one cell at a time in the direction indicated;

★ using the keyboard PgUp (Page up) and PgDn (Page down) keys to move a screen height at a time, up or down;

★ holding the keyboard Ctrl (Control) key down, whilst using the left or right arrow keys to move a screen width at a time;

★ using a 'mouse'.

There are a number of other shorthand ways of moving the cursor around the spreadsheet, but these are more likely to vary between spreadsheet types, and so will not be described here.

## Entering number and text

Numbers, calculations, cell addresses, text and special functions can be put into any cell by simply placing the cursor on the cell where they are required, typing them, and pressing the Enter or Return key (Enter and Return are the same thing).

Some spreadsheets need an initial character to designate the entry in some way, for instance, using Lotus 1-2-3 the calculation B1 + B2 + B3 in Example 3.1 is entered as + B1 + B2 + B3, the first + tells Lotus 1-2-3 that this is a calculation and not text. Excel uses an equals sign "=" as a prefix.

**Note:** Generally, initial characters will not be included in the book, because they do vary between spreadsheet types.

**Note:** In the book, characters that are to be entered are presented in the text as **bold characters**.

★ **EX31**   Try moving the cursor around, and changing some numbers, or entering some new ones.

## Column width

★ The width of a column is described by the number of characters or figures it can contain. Each column width can be set to accommodate as many figures or characters as are needed. If the cells to the right of a cell that contains text are empty, any characters more than the width of the cell will simply spill over them.

## Basic arithmetic

Calculations using addition, subtraction, multiplication and division are entered exactly as they would be written on paper, using the keyboard symbols + – * / respectively. They can be entered as:

★ Numbers only:                  **(3 + 10 – 4)/2**

   or

★ Cell addresses only:     **(B6 + B7 – C2)/E14**

   or

★ Mixed:                          **(3 + B7 – 4)/E14**

## Copying cell contents

Spreadsheets very often need calculations in several places that are identical in form, but which refer to different cells. For instance, in Example 3.1, the calculations for the totals from left to right are B1 + B2 + B3, C1 + C2 + C3 and D1 + D2 + D3. Now, whilst it is an easy matter to individually enter just these three calculations, it would clearly be very time consuming and tedious to type and enter them across a large number of columns.

Spreadsheets have a copying facility that enables the contents of a cell to be copied as many times as are needed, and what's more, they can automatically adjust any cell addresses during the copying process.

So if, for instance, in Example 3.1, the 'Totals' calculation was also wanted in cells E5 to H5, it is only necessary to instruct the spreadsheet to copy the contents of cell D5 into the range E5 to H5, and the correct changes to the formulae will be automatically made. Thus the contents of cells E5 to H5 will then be E1 + E2 + E3, F1 + F2 + F3, G1 + G2 + G3 and H1 + H2 + H3 respectively.

---

★**EX31**   Copy cell D5 to E5:H5, and try entering numbers in any or all of cells E1,E2,E3, F1,F2,F3, G1,G2,G3, H1,H2,H3.

---

**Note:** Cell ranges will be shown as the first and last in the series, with a colon between. For example, E5:H5 means all of the cells within the range, in this case E5, F5, G5, and H5. Spreadsheets use either this, or E5..H5, as conventions for ranges, although most will also accept a single full stop, or 'point' as a range separator when they are being entered.

## Functions

Spreadsheet programs provide a very large number of ready made functions, designed to simplify and minimise construction of both commonly used calculations, and those for very specific purposes.

**Table 3.1   The principal spreadsheet function types**

| | |
|---|---|
| ■ Arithmetic | ■ Trigonometric |
| ■ Statistical | ■ String |
| ■ Financial | ■ Index |
| ■ Logical | ■ Calendar and time |

Whilst some of the functions are likely to be used in virtually all spreadsheets, the vast majority are not required for budgeting. Nevertheless it is worth mentioning examples of all of the principal types to give some idea of what sort of things they are, and of the variety available.

## Arithmetic

SQRT(value)                     Square root of *value*.

ROUND(value,places)             *Value* rounded to number of *places*.

## Trigonometric

SIN(value)                      Sine of *value*.

PI                              Gives the value of Pi ($\pi$).

## Statistical

SUM(list)                       Sum of the values in *list*.

AVERAGE(list)                   The average (mean) of *list*.

## Text

RIGHT(string,n)                 Last *n* characters of *string*.

LEN(string)                     Length of *string*.

**Note:** A 'string' is any number of characters that are not being treated as values for calculation purposes, typically these are text labels like 'Totals' in Example 3.1.

## Financial

NPV (rate, value 1, value 2, ...) Net present value

SLN(cost,salvage,life)          Straight-line depreciation for one period.

## Index

CHOOSE(x,v0,v1,... .,vn)        The xth value from the list of values.

COLUMNS(range)                  Number of columns in *range*.

## Logical

IF(condition,x,y)               x if *condition* is True, y if *condition* is False.

OR(value 1,value 2)             True if either value is True; otherwise, False.

## Calendar and time

NOW                             System date and time.

DATE(dd,mm,yy)                  Date value of a specified date.

Most functions have a similar format – the name of the function before an opening bracket, the cell or range(s) of cells the function is to be applied to, then a closing bracket. Some spreadsheets require a special character before the function, for instance, Lotus 1–2–3 needs a preceding '@' character, Excel an equals '=' sign.

One of the most commonly used functions is SUM, and so it's a helpful one to look at more closely in a practical illustration.

Consider two columns of five figures in cells B7 to B11 and E7 to E11 that require totalling in cells B13 and E13, respectively.

One way to add the figures in column B is to type the calculation into B13 like this:

**B7 + B8 + B9 + B10 + B11**

That will certainly work, and it wouldn't take long to type it in as there only five figures. But suppose it were 20, or even a hundred figures – that would be an enormous amount of typing with a very high probability of error. The SUM function eliminates the need for all the typing, and has some other advantages as well which we will look at later.

SUM totals the contents of all of the cells within the *range* in its brackets, so putting **SUM(E7:E11)** in cell E13 will give the same result as adding each cell individually.

Example 3.2 (see opposite) shows the two identical columns of figures. The formulae shown in square brackets are the contents of the totals in cells B13 and E13.

> **Note:** There are some conventions in Example 3.2 that will be used elsewhere in the book. Square brackets embrace anything that is for explanation only, and not part of the spreadsheet.

Changes to any of the numbers in column E of Example 3.2 will still be reflected by the total SUM(E7:E11) of course, in exactly the same way as the formulae B7 + B8 + B9 + B10 + B11 for column B totals.

## Copying a function

Copying the formulae SUM(E7:E11) to other columns will, just as before, automatically adjust the cell addresses.

> ★**EX32**   Copy SUM(E7:E11) from cell E13 to cell F13, it will adjust to SUM(F7:F11). Put some numbers in cells F7 – F11.

**Note:** from now on I'll simply refer to cell addresses by their location, and drop the world 'cell'.

## Example 3.2 (∗EX32)  The SUM function

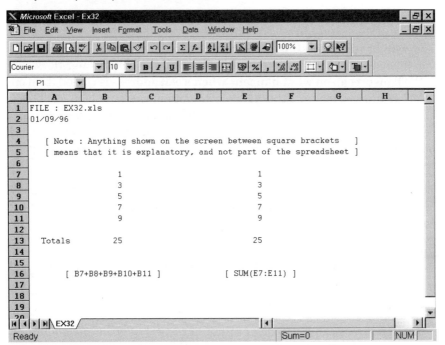

35

Until now totals have been positioned at the bottom of columns of figures, but there is no reason why, so far as the spreadsheet is concerned, a formulae should not be placed, or indeed repeated, anywhere. For example, suppose the totals for columns B and E in Example 3.2 were also wanted at the top right hand of the screen, one above the other.

This can be achieved by repeating the formulae for the totals, or by simply entering the cell addresses of the totals in the cell where they are wanted. The first way just repeats the calculations, the second displays whatever is in the cell referred to, and is probably the easiest and best method in most circumstances.

We'll try both methods.

For the first, there are two ways of repeating a formulae elsewhere, either retyping the calculation at the new location, or by copying it from the original location.

Copying is the very much easier and preferred way of course, but the automatic adjustment of cell addresses, when a formulae is copied, must be inhibited. All spreadsheets have a way of creating or copying what are known as *absolute addresses*, that is cell addresses that will not change or adjust to a new location under any circumstances.

We'll look at absolute cell addresses in more detail before copying the totals to the top right of the screen.

## Absolute addresses

The way in which a cell address can be made absolute is common to all spreadsheets. It looks complicated, but is actually very straightforward.

We'll just recap on what happens when a cell address is copied from one location to another and the address is automatically adjusted. This is known as *relative addressing*, because the adjustment is based on the relative position of the new location to the old. Simply put, if a cell address is copied two columns to the right, the column part of the address will increase by two columns.

★ Thus if cell address B2 is used in a formulae somewhere, and the formulae is copied two columns right, the address B2 in it will increase by two columns, from B to D, making the new address D2.

★ Similarly, if the same formulae is copied two rows down, the address B2 will increase by two rows, from 2 to 4, making the new address B4.

★ Finally, if the formulae is copied to a location two columns to the right, *and* two rows down, the address B2 will adjust to D4.

A cell address can be made absolute in respect of either its column, or its row, or both. Placing a '$' before either the column or row part of a cell address makes that part absolute.

For instance, $B2 makes the column absolute, B$2 makes the row absolute, and $B$2 makes both the column and the row absolute.

## Copying absolute addresses

★ If the address is $B$2, wherever it is copied to, it will still be $B$2.

★ Or if it is $B2, the column will always remain the same, but the row will adjust relative to its new position.

★ It works in exactly the same way in ranges, SUM($B$2:$B$3) will be unaltered wherever it is copied to, and SUM($B$2:B3) will adjust only in its second, B3, part.

★**EX33A**    Copy B13 to H2 as an absolute address. Enter E13 at H3. Put labels
in F2 and F3 to identify which is which.

★ Now whatever happens to the figures in column B and column E will be
reflected by the totals at their foot, and at the top right of the screen in
H2 and H3.

**Example 3.3a (★EX33a)  Two ways of repeating the column totals**

# Inserting and deleting rows and columns

There are all sorts of reasons for wanting to insert or delete rows and
columns, not the least being errors, or changes of mind, if my own
experience is anything to go by!

It is very easy to insert or delete rows and columns, after which the
spreadsheet will automatically relabel the whole spreadsheet's rows and
columns so that they still run contiguously.

Furthermore, it will also automatically and immediately adjust all
existing cell addresses to their new locations.

Let's see what happens if a new row is inserted above the existing row
9, in Example 3.3b (page 38).

> **★EX33A**    Place the cursor anywhere on row 9, and insert a row.

So far so good, there is now an extra row, the rest of the rows have been renumbered accordingly, and the totals are still correct.

But what if figures are now put into the newly created cells B9 and E9? Let's put 100 into each.

### Example 3.3b (★EX33b)  Inserting an extra row

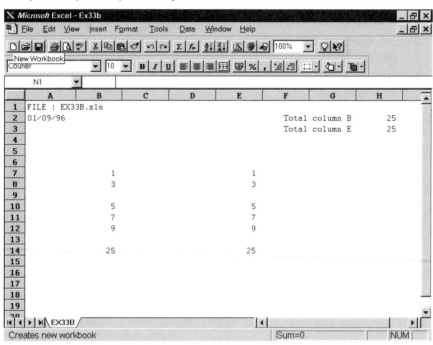

> **★EX33C**    Enter 100 in B9 and E9.

Now, what's happened? The total for column E is correct, but the column B total hasn't picked up the additional 100.

In Example 3.3c (see opposite), inspection of the total formulae in B14 (below it in Example 3.3c) shows why this is. The spreadsheet has adjusted the formulae, but it doesn't include the new row 9, because it hasn't been told to.

But, looking at the formulae in E9, however, (below it in Example 3.3c), here is another major advantage of using the SUM function. The last address in the range has adjusted, correctly of course, to E12. Clearly then, the new row 9 is included in the range E7:E12, and the sum is therefore still correct.

So the SUM function enables additional rows and columns to be inserted whilst the integrity of their calculation is maintained.

It also minimises the risk of unwittingly creating formulae that probably don't do what is actually wanted, as in B14.

*EX 33    If Row 9 had been deleted instead, the SUM function in E14 would still have worked properly, but the 'addition of individual cells' version in B14 wouldn't even have given an answer at all, it would have displayed an error message, such as #REF!

**Example 3.3c (*EX33c)  The effect of a new row on the different ways of adding a column of figures**

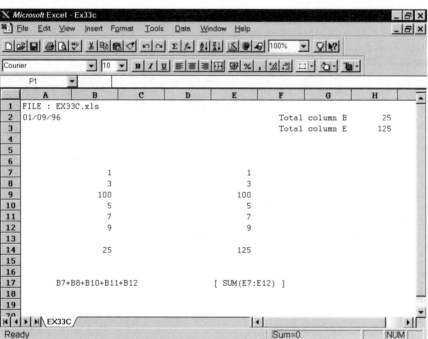

Inspection of the formulae would show that the position in the formulae where B9 had been, has been replaced with an error message, like this for instance: B7 + B8+ #REF! + B10 + B11.

## Formatting the presentation

Formatting is concerned with the appearance of the display, both on the screen and when printed on paper. It has no effect whatever on the calculations.

There are several formatting facilities, of which one is column width, mentioned earlier. The rest are principally concerned with the presentation of text (labels) and figures.

*Justification* refers to the presented position of the contents of a cell, within it. Text, figures and the result of any calculation can be justified to the left or to the right, or centred within the cell. Most spreadsheets have a default format of text left justified, and figures right justified. Whilst it is comparatively rare that the justification of figures needs to be changed, it is frequently required for text. For example, suppose the abbreviated month labels – Jan, Feb, Mar and Apr – were wanted at the head of their columns.

### Example 3.4a (∗EX34a) Month headings – left justified

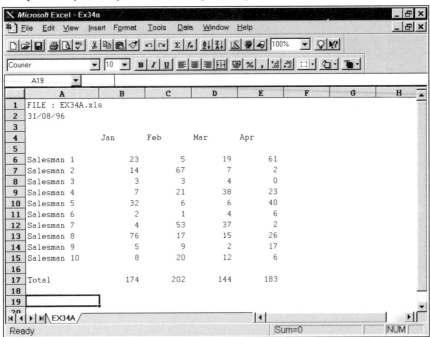

Example 3.4a (★ **EX34A**) shows a sales forecast model for a number of sales-men. Note that column A has been widened to accommodate the labels.

I have put the month labels and figures in without changing any for-matting arrangements, and they have defaulted to text left and figures right. There is so much misalignment between the month headings and the figures that it is quite difficult to see which belong to which, especially lower down the spreadsheet.

The solution is to format the text headings to right justification. Formats can be applied to individual cells, or to an entire row or column. In this case, because row 4 will contain only headings, I'll format the row to right justify.

---

**★EX34A**    Format row 4 to right justify.

---

In Example 3.4b (below) the headings are now properly aligned with the figures, and consequently much easier to read.

*Numerical format* refers to the way in which figures are displayed, remember, none of the following affects the accuracy of any calculations.

## Example 3.4b (★EX34b) Month headings – right justified

| | A | B | C | D | E |
|---|---|---|---|---|---|
| 1 | FILE : EX34B.xls | | | | |
| 2 | 31/08/96 | | | | |
| 3 | | | | | |
| 4 | | Jan | Feb | Mar | Apr |
| 5 | | | | | |
| 6 | Salesman 1 | 23 | 5 | 19 | 61 |
| 7 | Salesman 2 | 14 | 67 | 7 | 2 |
| 8 | Salesman 3 | 3 | 3 | 4 | 0 |
| 9 | Salesman 4 | 7 | 21 | 38 | 23 |
| 10 | Salesman 5 | 32 | 6 | 6 | 40 |
| 11 | Salesman 6 | 2 | 1 | 4 | 6 |
| 12 | Salesman 7 | 4 | 53 | 37 | 2 |
| 13 | Salesman 8 | 76 | 17 | 15 | 26 |
| 14 | Salesman 9 | 5 | 9 | 2 | 17 |
| 15 | Salesman 10 | 8 | 20 | 12 | 6 |
| 16 | | | | | |
| 17 | Total | 174 | 202 | 144 | 183 |

Suppose we have a calculation of 250000 divided by 52. That's 25000/52, which is 4807.69230769 to eight decimal places. But it is unlikely in budget applications that a display like this would be wanted. We are more likely to require two decimal places, which is 4807.69 rounded down.

Just about any presentation can be produced on a spreadsheet, a selection is displayed on Figure 3.4. The column used for the figures is set to a width of 15 characters, and the figures themselves are left justified for clarity.

## Graphs (charts)

Graphs are sometimes called 'charts' by software manufacturers.

There are many instances in budgeting and forecasting when graphical representation of some of the figures can be very useful indeed. All spreadsheets can produce graphs, some of them to an extremely high level of sophistication.

42

**Figure 3.4 Examples of numerical formats**

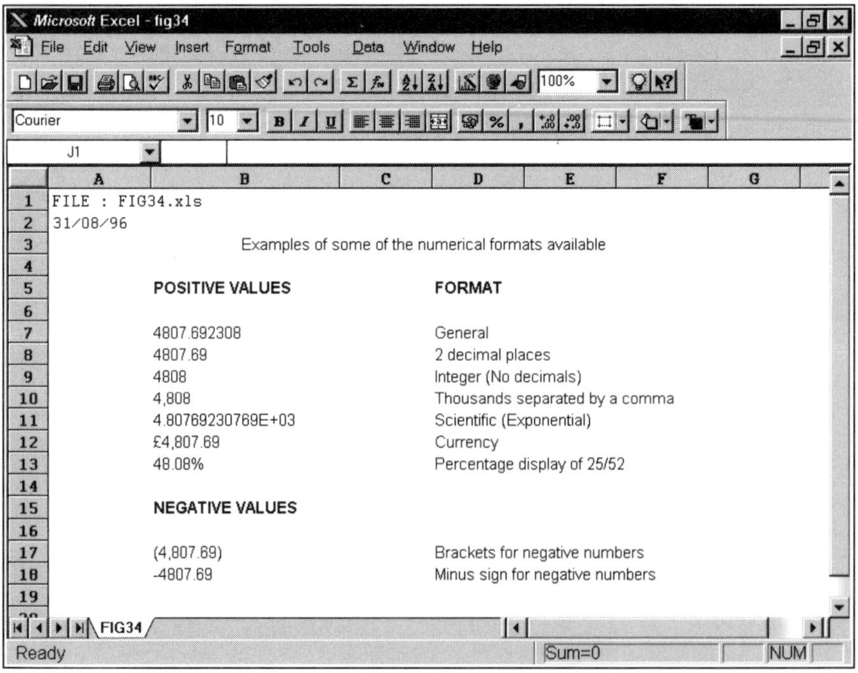

**Figure 3.5 Examples of spreadsheet graphs**

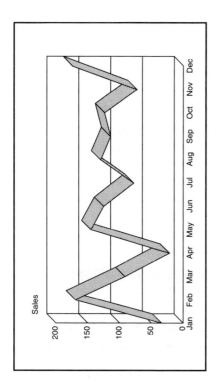

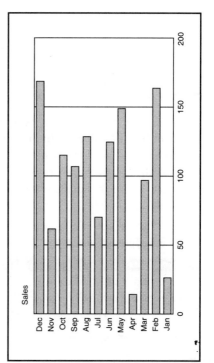

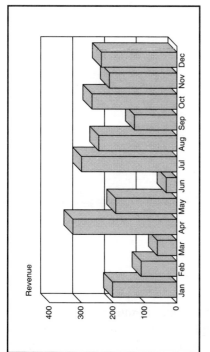

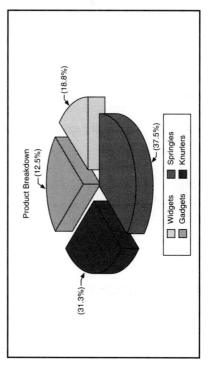

43

The way in which graphs are created is very different for each type of spreadsheet, and so it has sufficed for our purpose to show some of the different types that most of them can produce – Figure 3.5 (see page 43).

# Ranges

A range, as it was used for example in the SUM function, is a block of cells that can be fully defined by its top left hand corner, and its bottom right-hand corner – see the upper example in Figure 3.6 (below). It is also permissible to combine two ranges and treat them as one for the purpose of functions – see the lower example in Figure 3.6.

**Figure 3.6 Spreadsheet ranges**

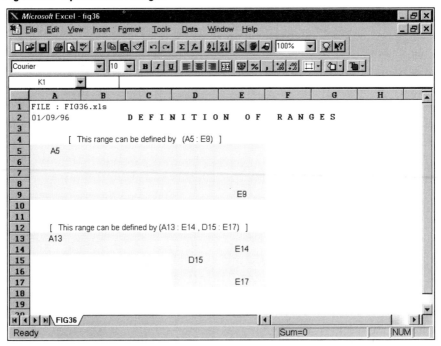

# Naming ranges

Ranges can be given names – literally any name you like. In Figure 3.7 (see opposite), the range in the upper example has been given the name SALES, and can then be referred to by name. So, instead of having to type

SUM(A5:E9), SUM(SALES) can be entered. In fact, having named a range, even if you do enter it typed in full, the spreadsheet will immediately replace the range with its name.

## Figure 3.7 Spreadsheet named ranges

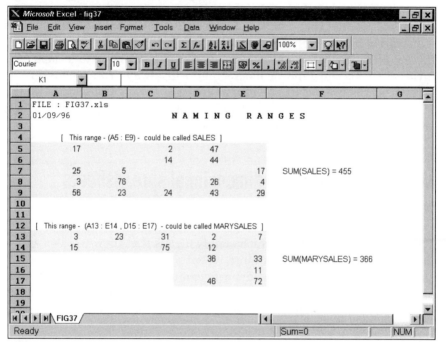

45

The principal advantages of using named ranges are that formulae are easier to construct, and easier to understand later on. For example, if the sum totals of sales for the months of January to December are required in various calculations, each of the totals can be named JANSALES, FEBSALES ... etc. Thereafter, in any formulae that requires them, instead of having to remember the cell addresses of the ranges, all you need to do is type the name(s). The first quarter's sales could be calculated simply by typing JANSALES + FEBSALES + MARSALES.

Obviously any calculations that look like this will be much more easily understood by anyone else, and by you as well when you look at the spreadsheet again, in detail, for the first time in 12 months! Named ranges have saved many a scratched head and premature baldness.

> With more recent versions of the major spreadsheet types, multi-page spreadsheets can be created, analogous to several pieces of paper, which can provide a third dimension.

## Macros

Don't be put off by this rather technical sounding term – simple macros are very easy indeed, and can sometimes be extremely useful.

A spreadsheet macro is nothing more than a means of 'recording' a sequence of operations, so that they can be automatically 'played back' when required – instead of having to type them all in again. Macros are especially useful for often repeated operations, or ones that are rather long and involved. A special kind of macro that will always run whenever the spreadsheet is 'loaded' can be also be created.

Most spreadsheets have excellent systems for 'learning' macros whilst you simply carry out the operation once.

## 46 | Multi-sheet and three-dimensional spreadsheets
■ ■ ■

Ordinary spreadsheets are analogous to a single piece of paper, or sheet. They are two dimensional, which simply means that there are two axes – the rows and columns. With more recent versions of the major spreadsheet types, multi-sheet spreadsheets can be created, analogous to several pieces of paper, which can provide a third dimension. This facility has many uses, for example, in the organisation of large spreadsheets or combining data from several departments or for several products.

Figure 3.8 (opposite) shows a multi-sheet spreadsheet with four sheets. Sheet 1 has formulae that sum the corresponding cells in each of the other sheets.

A three-dimensional model can also be created by 'linking' two or more completely separate spreadsheets together. This is how the example forecast will be built in Chapter 6.

**Figure 3.8  A linked multi-sheet spreadsheet**

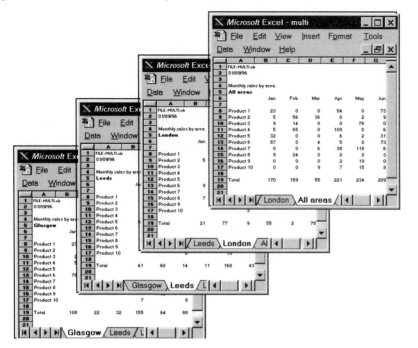

## Summary

In this chapter we have seen that:

■ the principle of computer spreadsheets is closely analogous to their paper equivalent, and that the intersection of columns and rows is called a cell, and is described by a letter and number known as a cell address;

■ calculations can be written into cells, and include figures, cell addresses and formulae;

■ explanatory or labelling text can be written into cells;

■ there is a very wide range of functions available in a spreadsheet, some of which make model construction easier, and others that provide for specialised requirements;

■ multi-page and three-dimensional spreadsheets can be created.

It would be impertinent and wrong to imply that the conventions and practices used in this book are the best ones, or that they are infallible. They have, however, been learned and developed from practical experience, and they do work.

# 4

# Spreadsheet techniques for budgeting and forecasting

A multitude of ways and means ■

Essential practices and conventions ■

Example forecasts ■

Examples of non-essential, but useful techniques ■

This chapter aims to deal with most of the spreadsheet techniques and principles that will be used in Part 3 for the construction of budget and cash flow forecasts.

# A multitude of ways and means
■ ■ ■

When using a spreadsheet, as with any highly flexible system, there are many different ways of achieving an objective.

It would be impertinent and wrong to imply that the conventions and practices used in this book are the best ones, or that they are infallible. They have, however, been learned and developed from practical experience, and they do work. By following them you will benefit from the myriad of mistakes I have made over the years, and thus more quickly develop your own 'style' and conventions.

The section below on *Essential practices and conventions* does mean just that. You will ignore them at your peril and certain regret, sooner or later. I know, because every one of them has caught me. Usually only once to be sure, but that was enough!

# Essential practices and conventions
■ ■ ■

These practices and conventions are to do with efficiency, the safe keeping of your work, accuracy, avoidance of errors and elimination of confusion. Adhering to them will minimise risk to your credibility, and enhance your reputation as a forecaster. Ignoring them will almost certainly result in your credibility taking a severe knock, and without doubt, one day, the complete loss of many hours of your work.

**There are two main ways of storing information, either on a *disc, or in memory*.**

Sometimes, but by no means always, these practices and conventions may take a little more time, but only a fraction of that which will otherwise be wasted.

## Regular saving

This is so important that a brief technical explanation of how information is stored and used by a computer is necessary. None of this detail is essential to being able to use a spreadsheet, but it will explain why regular saving is crucial.

There are two main ways of storing information, either on a *disc,* or *in memory*.

There are two kinds of disc, a *hard* disc which is usually a fixed and sealed unit inside the computer's case, and a *floppy* disc which can be removed from the computer and stored or used elsewhere.

The essential feature of any disc is that it is permanent means of storage, it works in a very similar way to an everyday audio or video cassette tape. Once information has been stored on a disc, with normal care, it is there for good. However, for many computer programs, including spreadsheets, disc storage is not suitable whilst they are being used. A more accessible method is needed – *memory*.

Memory – often referred to as RAM (Random Access Memory) – is a much more accessible and convenient means of storage for a computer. Please note, however, information is only stored in memory temporarily.

When a spreadsheet is used, the computer automatically copies all of the information it needs from the disc to the memory. Therefore, any changes made to a spreadsheet exist *only in memory* until you *copy it back to the disc*. This copying back process is known as 'saving' or 'keeping'.

If power to the computer is lost, either deliberately or accidentally, anything in memory at the time is lost irrevocably.

Also, if something else is copied into memory, it may well replace the current contents if there is either insufficient memory for both, or they are not able to coexist.

Now all of this may seem very frightening. Is it really so easy to lose a lot of work in this way? Yes, it is! However, it is also very easy indeed to avoid it, and all good spreadsheets give a prominent warning if you are in danger of losing work.

The simple way to minimise the risk of losing your work is to 'save' it frequently and regularly whenever you are creating or changing anything. There is no absolute rule on frequency, but every two or three minutes will suffice in most cases. It only takes a couple of keystrokes and two or three seconds, and after a while you will find that you are doing it almost as naturally as breathing.

Is saving every two or three minutes taking safety and security too far? Just consider how long it will take to rethink and recreate what you have done since the last time your work was saved.

## Backing up

There is an adage in computing that 'information hasn't been entered until it has been backed up'. 'Backing up' means making another copy of your work.

There are two main ways in which information on a hard or floppy disc can be lost. Firstly technical failure – all technical systems *will* go wrong one day. This means, for instance that a hard or floppy disc could fail in a way that would make it impossible to recover any of the information on it. Secondly, non-technical losses occur through theft or fire.

All of this means that *back-up copies* must be kept, preferably either in a fireproof safe, or at another location, or both.

There are several ways of backing up, the main ones being:

■ copies on floppy discs;

■ copies on a tape using a tape streamer;

■ copies on another computer.

For budgeting and forecasting, an adequate, simple and quick method is the first. Just make copies of the spreadsheets on floppy discs and store them somewhere safe. A daily or 'end of session' back up in this way will usually be sufficient. If you already have more stringent data security measures, that's fine.

## Version numbers, date and time stamps

You are responsible for preparing a financial plan for a new project and presenting it to the Board of Directors. Over many days you and your colleagues work late into the night producing more and more refined versions of the plan. Then, in that inevitable, and, certainly unplanned, last minute rush to finalise the presentation, the wrong version is picked up by someone for binding into the folios that will be distributed to board members.

In this case no permanent damage will be done, except to your career. It will simply be a matter of a very red face when those sitting around the table notice that what you are presenting on the screen is different to what they have in front of them.

There are many other scenarios where such a mistake can have the most severe consequences for the company, but there are two simple ways of avoiding them – *version numbering and date and time stamping*.

*Version numbering* is nothing more than giving your spreadsheet a file name that can be changed in some sort of sequence whenever a significant change is made to its structure. For example, starting with PLAN01 as a file name, this can be incremented to PLAN02, and so on, providing 99 discrete identities.

*Date and time stamping* consists of including in your spreadsheet the functions that automatically present the current system date and time. There is no reason whatever for not including both whilst development is ongoing. It only takes seconds, just once, to put these functions into their cells, after that it is all fully automatic. Whenever the spreadsheet is saved, it will retain the current date and time.

> On a spreadsheet, before you know it, you have merrily overwritten those elegant formulae you were so proud of, and which took half an hour to work out.

Both methods should be used. Version numbering is useful for ensuring that the correct computer file is being handled, during back up for instance. Date and time stamping is invaluable on paper copies during development, and for regularly repeated reports. In the second case, once development is finished, the date alone may be sufficient.

## Cell protection

*Cell protection* is a simple means of preventing the contents of a cell being changed accidentally, though an easy and deliberate action can remove the protection when required.

Once you become accustomed to your spreadsheet, and your fingers start to move swiftly and smoothly over the keyboard – **watch out!**

Overconfidence on the keyboard, as in many other skills, can be disastrous. On a spreadsheet, before you know it, you have merrily overwritten those elegant formulae you were so proud of, and which took half an hour to work out. OK – if you were 'saving' every two or three minutes, you can recover the work. But you will still have lost at least five minutes. Protecting those cells on which work is finished will prevent accidental overwriting.

More critically, especially on larger spreadsheets, you will find that you have a mixture of cells, some of which contain formulae, and others that are intended to receive keyboard entered variables. Whilst there are ways of organising the spreadsheet to minimise confusion about which are which, a sure method is to protect the cells that are not to be changed either during development or in normal day-to-day operations.

Finally, more often than not only a small part of a spreadsheet model can be seen on the screen at any one time. It is thus extremely easy to delete rows or columns that you think are unused, only to find that there were entries in cells not in the current screen view.

Protecting cells foils accidental deletion of data in this way, simply because any row or column that has protected cells in it cannot be deleted.

53

# Check sum

Despite the ease with which formulae can be copied, or perhaps because of it and that old enemy 'over confidence' again, it can happen that somewhere in a series of cells there are formulae errors. I have created these sort of errors most frequently when trying out a new sequence of calculations on just one column. Then once having got it right, intended to copy all of the amended formulae across the rest of the columns in the model, but have forgotten to copy one of the revised rows.

Check sums, or variations on them, are a useful way of showing when such an error has occurred. Their principle is based on the notion that almost all results can be calculated in more than one way. For instance, in Example 4.1 (★ **EX41**) below, the grand totals '276' have been calculated by the sum of the individual totals above them, so these are column-based sums. But they could just as easily be calculated from the individual totals to their left, which are row-based sums.

### Example 4.1 (★EX41)  Using a check sum to detect errors

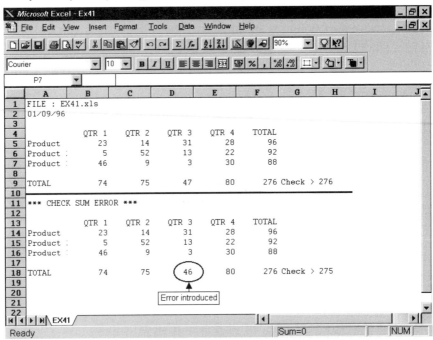

So why not have both? Perhaps use the column-based sum in the 'usual' place, in this case F9 and F18, and put the row version somewhere nearby. I have used H9 and H18. If there are no errors, both row and column totals will be identical, and it isn't even necessary to keep on comparing them manually – the spreadsheet can do it for you.

If, in the lower part of the screen in Example 4.1 (★ **EX41**), I 'accidentally' overwrite the formulae in D18 with a number that is one less than the calculated value, the column version of the grand total still gives the correct answer '276', but the row-based check version just to its right produces '275', of course.

In this example, I have also provided an IF function that flags up its message only when the two versions of the calculation are not the same. The IF function in A11, for example, is:

**IF(F18<>H18",*** CHECK SUM ERROR ***","")**

There is also a similar function in A3 to flag errors for the model at the top of the screen.

| | |
|---|---|
| ★**EX41** | Try overwriting a formulae in the upper model and see the check sum message appear. |

55

A similar principle can be applied to just about any set of calculations, and the bigger or more complex the spreadsheet, the more essential a set of check sums to provide integrity validation becomes.

## Automatic recalculation

Recalculating a larger spreadsheet model can take several seconds. Because of this, most spreadsheet types have a facility for switching off automatic recalculation so that when a series of keyboard entries are being made it isn't necessary to wait for each recalculation before making the next entry.

Also, some spreadsheets have a facility whereby recalculation will immediately stop when any key is pressed, this means that auto-recalculation can be left permanently switched on, even when entering a series of data on a large model.

Now, these are very useful facilities – but, be careful. When auto-recalculation is switched off, or stopped, the effect of any changes you make will not be reflected elsewhere in the spreadsheet until you activate a recalculation – usually with key F9. In either case the spreadsheet will warn you if calculations are outstanding by displaying a warning message somewhere on the screen. Make a habit of glancing at that display, and pressing F9 before reading or printing the spreadsheet.

# Example forecasts

■   ■   ■

Every company's forecast structure will be different, and choosing the main elements and subheadings from a financial point of view will be discussed in detail in Part 3.

In this chapter, simple sales, budget, and cash flow forecasting models are used only for illustrating the use of spreadsheets.

Therefore, the main elements and subheadings used in them, though broadly appropriate, are not intended to be proforma. For the same reason, the main elements and subheadings used are neither explained nor justified – all will be revealed in Part 3!

Now, some people advocate 'getting your thoughts straight' on paper first, so that all you have to do then is type in the finalised layout. Well … yes, you can do that of course, but I have never yet seen a new layout that wasn't changed very soon after it was started. In my view, it's easier to draft a layout on the spreadsheet in the first place, things can be moved around much more easily than pencil on paper can, and better still, you will immediately see whether the layout *looks* right as well.

In the examples that follow, methods and recommended techniques are introduced as the need for them arises, thus the most fundamental are among the earliest to make an appearance. Once each has been described, although probably used again in a later example, its purpose or method of implementation will not be repeated. This means that if you address the examples out of order, you may need to refer to an earlier one for an explanation on some point of detail.

Where functions not previously described are used, they are given in both Excel and Lotus 1-2-3 format.

## Sales forecast example

This example illustrates the following techniques:

- file naming;
- date and time stamping;
- hidden columns;
- justifying text left, right and centre;
- cell protection;
- expanding a column width to fit the text;
- spare rows used to allow for later expansion;
- entering and checking formulae in one column initially;

- copying a range of formulae across columns;
- year totals, using 'IF' to exclude unused rows;
- check sums and warning flags;
- building in 'month-on-month' sales growth;
- integer format and elimination of unwanted decimal places.

---

Examples ★**EX42–EX46** are a progression in which all of the steps shown have been completed. Try using one to create the next in the series yourself.

---

## Steps – for Example 4.2

Using a blank spreadsheet:

1 Choose a file name for the model and enter it as text in A1. Unless you are using Windows 95 a file name can consist of up to eight characters before the dot, and up to three after the dot. Any characters after the dot are known as the file name extension. All spreadsheets automatically allocate a default extension, and it is best to accept it. Any alphabetical or numeric character can be used in a file name, but spaces are not allowed. Whilst some special characters can be used, others cannot, so it is easiest to stick to alpha-numeric only. Windows 95 file names can be longer and include spaces.

2 Enter the function for the current system date in A2. It will also be necessary to set the cell to a date format.
3 Enter the function for the current time in A3. It will also be necessary to set the cell to a time format.
4 Enter titles for the spreadsheet at its top.
5 Enter month and year total headings in columns B to N. In the example columns G to L have been hidden so that the headings for December and the Year Total can be seen.
6 Format the headings to the right so that they will line up with the numbers to be entered later.
7 Save the model using the file name you have put in A1.

## Steps – for Example 4.3

1 Enter the row headings as text, don't worry at this stage that some don't fit within the column width.
2 The *spare* rows above the totals allow insertion of additional rows below the existing titles without the need to modify sum formulae. Providing that any column sum formula include the 'spare' row, and

## Example 4.2 (∗EX42)  First steps building a sales forecast

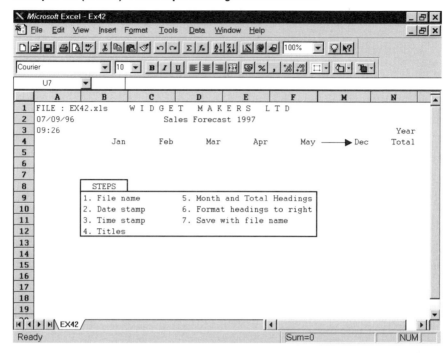

## Example 4.3 (∗EX43)  Entering and justifying the row headings

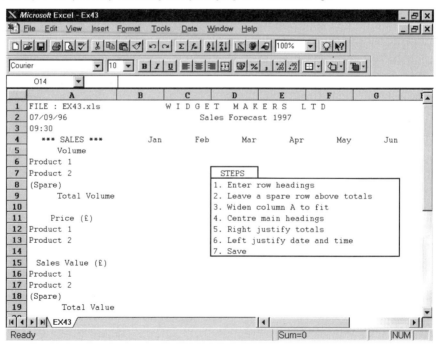

## Example 4.4 (∗EX44) Entering and testing the formulae

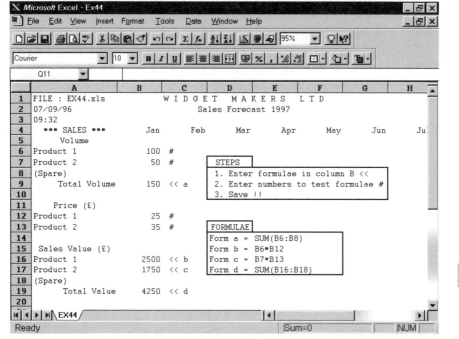

that new rows are inserted above it, the sum formula will automatically adjust to accommodate them.

3 Widen column A to fit the longest row heading.

4 Centre the main headings – '∗∗∗ SALES ∗∗∗', 'Volume', 'Price (£)', and 'Sales Value (£)'.

5 Right justify the totals headings – 'Total Volume' and 'Total Value'.

6 The date and time may now look rather odd if they are right justified. If so, left justify them.

7 Save again !!

## Steps – for Example 4.4

1 Enter formulae, in column B only, at positions « a, b, c and d as shown on Example 4.4 (see above). Note that the 'spare' rows are included in the formulae.

2 Enter some sales quantities and prices, in column B only, at the positons indicated by #. Check that results at positions « a, b, c and d are correct. If they aren't, the formulae must be wrong. Check and correct them.

3 Save!!!

## Steps – for Example 4.5

**Note:** In the illustration for Example 4.5, months Mar – Nov have been hidden so that the right hand end of the model can be seen.

1 Copy the range B6:B19 to M6.
2 Entering the year totals. This could be done by putting SUM(B6:M6), and then copying it to rows 7 to 19.

**★EX45**   If you try it in that way,the rows with nothing in them, such as 8 and 10, will of course present the result '0'.

To avoid getting a '0' result where none is needed, use an 'IF' funtion like this – **IF(SUM(B6:M6)<>0,SUM(B6:M6),"")**.

In words the function means – *if* the sum of B6:M6 does not equal 0, *then* sum B6:M6, *else* display blank text.

Copy the function to rows 7 to 19, and only those sums that are greater than zero will display a result.

3 A year sum of rows 12 and 13 is meaningless, as they are the price rows. Delete the entries in N12 and N13.
4 Save !!! (I won't say this any more … although you never know!).

**★EX45**   Check that the model works as you would expect by changing a volume figure and a price figure.

6 Now we'll put a couple of check sums in for 'Total Volume' and 'Total Value'. Both of these are already calculated by summing the rows, so the check sum could be carried out on column N instead. In O9 enter SUM(N6:N8), and then copy it to O19 so that **SUM(N16:N18)** appears there.

It will be useful to be able to display an error warning in a more obvious position on the screen, perhaps near the top left. One way to achieve this for more than one check sum is like this:

7 At P9 (left of 'a' on the illustration), enter **IF(N9<>O9,1,"")**. This means – *if* the value of cell N9 does not equal the value of cell O9, *then* display '1', *else* display blank text. Now copy the formulae to P19 (left of 'b' on the illustration) so that **IF(N19<>O19,1,"")** appears there. Now, if an error occurs whereby either of the check sums does not equal its partner, '1' will appear beside it in column P.
8 The sum of the range P6:P19 will equal '0' if there are no errors, and so we can easily check that one or more errors exist by testing the sum

of that range. It may be a useful aid to understanding the formulae later if a named range is created for this test, so give the range P6:P19 a name. I have called it ERRANGE in the example.

9 Now all that is needed is the warning flag. I have put it in B3 as **IF(SUM(ERRANGE)>0,"!!! CHECK SUM ERROR !!!","")**, which means – *if* the sum of ERRANGE is greater than '0', *then* display !!! CHECK SUM ERROR !!!, *else* display blank text.

---

★ **EX45**   Try over-writing one of the 'Total Volume' or 'Total Value' formulae, and see the error warning appear in B3.

---

**Example 4.5 (★EX45) Copying figures for the year, row year totals and checks sums**

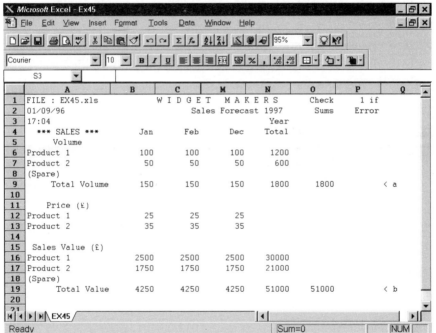

We now have a spreadsheet model that can, for example:

■ show the value per product or in total, for any product sales volume we care to enter, for a single month or for the whole year;

■ be used to examine the sales value impact of price changes.

It is also very easy to build into the model some regular changes. For example, suppose that a sales growth of 5 per cent and 10 per cent month on month are expected for Product 1 and Product 2, respectively.

Formulae can be created so that only one sales volume figure need be entered for each product.

## Steps – for Example 4.6

1 Unprotect cells C6 to M6, and C7 to M7.

2 Make the formulae in C6 **B6*1.05** and in C7 **B7*1.1**. The cursor in Example 4.6 (see below) is on C6, so that you can see the formulae it contains – near the bottom centre.

3 Copy both formulae to column M. Remember that you can copy both in one operation.

4 If the results of calculations are now displayed to several decimal places you will probably want to reset them to whole numbers (integers).

5 Now just enter the starting sales volume figure for each product in B6 and B7, the recalculated sales volume and resulting sales values can now be seen.

## Example 4.6 (∗EX46) Building in 'test' sales growth

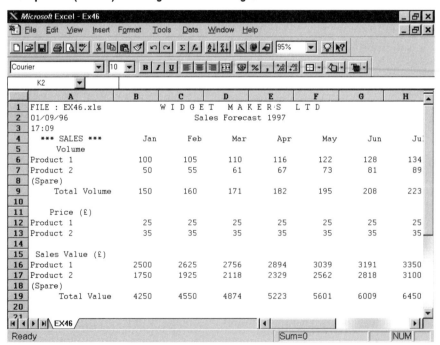

Now that we have a *sales forecast*, we'll go on to build a *budget forecast* based on the sales.

---

**Note:** Where spreadsheet models are larger than can be seen on a single screen, illustrations will not be presented as computer screen images.

---

# Budget forecast example

This example illustrates linking between files.

### Steps – for Example 4.7

Using a blank spreadsheet:

1 Create a spreadsheet model for a 12-month period, including year totals.

2 Add the row headings given below, justify them as shown, and set the width of column A to fit.

3 Enter in column B only:
   Formulae as shown.
   Direct costs/item as shown.
   Overheads as shown.

4 Copy all formulae and values through to column M (December).

5 Enter 'Vehicle' costs: £15,000 in March.

6 Enter 'Machinery' costs: £5,000 in May, £25,000 in October.

The model as it now stands will calculate the total *capital* and *overhead* costs, and their combined total. But there won't be any *direct* costs included yet, because they are derived by multiplying the *direct cost/ item by the product volumes* – and these haven't yet been entered.

It would be a fairly easy to print out the *product volume* figures from the *sales* forecast, and enter them month by month into the *budget* forecast. But that is the hard way, and of course they would then need to be re-entered every time the sales forecast changed. And sales forecasts have a habit of changing!

Clearly it would be better to link the product volume figures in the sales forecast directly to the budget forecast. Linking simply means putting in one cell – say B5, the address of another – say B46. B5 will then display the contents of B46.

## Example 4.7 (★EX47)  Budget forecast row headings and formulae

```
              |              A              ||      B      ||

    1    FILE : Name
    2    Date Stamp
    3    Time Stamp
    4
    5                                              Jan
    6                  SALES
    7    Volume - Product 1
    8    Volume - Product 2
    9    (Spare)
   10                          Total      SUM(B7:B9)
   11
   12    Value
   13
   14          CAPITAL COSTS
   15    Vehicles
   16    Machinery
   17    (Spare)
   18                      Total (A)      SUM(B15:B17)
   19
   20       DIRECT COSTS / ITEM
   21    Product 1                              5
   22    Product 2                              6
   23    (Spare)
   24
   25          DIRECT COSTS
   26    (Vol x Cost / Item)
   27    Product 1                          B7*B21
   28    Product 2                          B8*B22
   29    (Spare)
   30                      Total (B)      SUM(B27:B29)
   31
   32          OVERHEADS
   33    Accommodation                          135
   34    Electricity                            120
   35    Gas                                     68
   36    Telephone                               70
   37    Salaries                              3500
   38    (Spare)
   39                      Total (C)      SUM(B33:B38)
   40
   41         TOTAL COSTS
   42         ( A + B + C )
   43                      Total (D)      B18+B30+B38
```

Three kinds of links can be created:

■ *Spreadsheet* – where one cell on a spreadsheet is linked to another on the same spreadsheet, as in the example of B5 and B46 above.

■ *Sheet* – where a cell on one sheet refers to a cell on another sheet of a multi-sheet spreadsheet.

■ *File* – where a cell on one spreadsheet file refers to a cell on a completely different spreadsheet file, even though the file referred to is not loaded into memory.

There are pros and cons for using any of these types to link product volumes between the sales and budget forecasts.

Spreadsheet links are very easy indeed to create, but they suffer from making any one model rather large and difficult to manage. In our present case it would mean combining the sales and budget forecasts on one spreadsheet model.

Sheet links make a larger model easier to manage by breaking it down to manageable chunks, but, as with spreadsheet links, they are not suitable for splitting up so that for instance two different people could maintain the sales and budget forecasts independently.

File links provide the best solution. Compact models can be created and maintained by different people, yet be linked so that any changes to one are reflected in the other.

This is how file links in the budget forecast can be used to pick up the product volumes from the sales forecast.

65

## Steps – for Example 4.8

1   Check the cell addresses of the product volumes in column B of the sales forecast (Example 4.6). They are B6 and B7 for Products 1 and 2, respectively.
2   In B7 (Volume – Product 1) of the budget forecast, link the files by entering the following:

> For Excel:          = **EX46!B6**
> For Lotus 1-2-3:     +<<**EX46**>>**B6**

Note that the syntax is simply:

■ For Excel – an = sign, followed by the name of the file referred to, followed by an exclamation mark, followed by the cell link required.
■ For Lotus 1-2-3 – a plus sign, followed by the file name enclosed by double angled brackets, followed by the cell link required.
3   Repeat Step 2 for Volume – Product 2. The formulae for Excel is =**EX46!B7**. Note that the direct costs for both products have now been calculated for January.
4   Copy both formulae across to December.

The total cost shown on the budget forecast now includes the direct costs, and any changes to the product volumes on the sales forecast will be automatically picked up by the budget forecast.

This principle of file linking will be used extensively in the cash flow forecast that follows.

### Example 4.8 (∗EX48) The budget linked to the sales forecast

| | A | B | C | D | E | F | G | H | I |
|---|---|---|---|---|---|---|---|---|---|
| 1 | FILE:EX48.xls | | WIDGET | MAKERS | LTD | | | | |
| 2 | 05/09/96 | | Budget Forecast - 1997 | | | | | | |
| 3 | 20:11 | | | | | | | | |
| 4 | | | | | | | | | |
| 5 | | Jan | Feb | Mar | Apr | May | Jun | Jul | Aug |
| 6 | SALES | | | | | | | | |
| 7 | Volume - Product 1 | 100 | 105 | 110 | 116 | 122 | 128 | 134 | 141 |
| 8 | Volume - Product 2 | 50 | 55 | 61 | 67 | 73 | 81 | 89 | 97 |
| 9 | (Spare) | | | | | | | | |
| 10 | Total | 150 | 160 | 171 | 182 | 195 | 208 | 223 | 238 |
| 11 | | | | | | | | | |
| 12 | Value | 4250 | 4550 | 4874 | 5223 | 5601 | 6009 | 6450 | 6928 |
| 13 | | | | | | | | | |
| 14 | CAPITAL COSTS | | | | | | | | |
| 15 | Vehicles | | | 15000 | | | | | |
| 16 | Machinery | | | | | 5000 | | | |
| 17 | (Spare) | | | | | | | | |
| 18 | Total (A) | 0 | 0 | 15000 | 0 | 5000 | 0 | 0 | 0 |
| 19 | | | | | | | | | |
| 20 | DIRECT COSTS /ITEM | | | | | | | | |
| 21 | Product 1 | 5 | 5 | 5 | 5 | 5 | 5 | 5 | 5 |
| 22 | Product 2 | 6 | 6 | 6 | 6 | 6 | 6 | 6 | 6 |
| 23 | (Spare) | | | | | | | | |
| 24 | | | | | | | | | |
| 2S | DIRECT COSTS | | | | | | | | |
| 26 | (Vol x Cost / Item) | | | | | | | | |
| 27 | Product 1 | 500 | 525 | 551 | 579 | 608 | 638 | 670 | 704 |
| 28 | Product 2 | 300 | 330 | 363 | 399 | 439 | 483 | 531 | 585 |
| 29 | (Spare) | | | | | | | | |
| 30 | Total (B) | 800 | 855 | 914 | 978 | 1047 | 1121 | 1202 | 1288 |
| 31 | | | | | | | | | |
| 32 | OVERHEADS | | | | | | | | |
| 33 | Accommodation | 135 | 135 | 135 | 135 | 135 | 135 | 135 | 135 |
| 34 | Electricity | 120 | 120 | 120 | 120 | 120 | 120 | 120 | 120 |
| 35 | Gas | 68 | 68 | 68 | 68 | 68 | 68 | 68 | 68 |
| 36 | Telephone | 70 | 70 | 70 | 70 | 70 | 70 | 70 | 70 |
| 37 | Salaries | 3500 | 3500 | 3500 | 3500 | 3500 | 3500 | 3500 | 3500 |
| 38 | (Spare) | | | | | | | | |
| 39 | Total (C) | 3893 | 3893 | 3893 | 3893 | 3893 | 3893 | 3893 | 3893 |
| 40 | | | | | | | | | |
| 41 | TOTAL COSTS | | | | | | | | |
| 42 | ( A + B + C ) | | | | | | | | |
| 43 | Total (D) | 800 | 855 | 15914 | 978 | 6047 | 1121 | 1202 | 1288 |

# Cash flow forecast example

This example:

■ consolidates the use of file linking;

■ shows how cash flow can be related to the budget forecast.

## Steps – for Example 4.9

Using a blank spreadsheet:

1 Create a spreadsheet model for a 12-month period, including year totals.
2 Add the row headings given below, justify them as shown, and set the width of column A to fit.

Now, because cash flow is wholly dependent, in this case, on the budget, the cash flow figures can be picked up directly from it using file links. But there are timing differences or offsets to take account of, and which, for this example, assumptions need to be made.

## Cash flow timing assumption

Cash from sales is received one month *after* the sale. That is, the cash from January sales in the budget will be shown as received in February on the cash flow, and so on.

3 January sales value is in B12 of the Budget (Example 4.8). To pick it up in February of the cash flow, link C8 of the cash flow (Example 4.9) to B12 of the budget (Example 4.8).

   Like this, in C8 enter:

   Excel:            =EX48!B12
   Lotus 1-2-3:      +<<EX48>>B12

   Copy to March and on through to December.

> **Note:** There will normally be sales from December in the previous budget that would be fed through to January, unless this is a new business.

## Cash flow timing assumption

The widget manufacturing cycle of two months means that parts must be acquired two months before sales. But the parts supplier provides one month's credit, and so the cash to pay for them goes out one month *before* the sale.

4 February Product 1 costs are in C27 of the budget (Example 4.8). To pick them up in January of the cash flow, link B24 of the cash flow (Example 4.9) to C27 of the budget (Example 4.8).

Like this, in B24 enter:

| | |
|---|---|
| Excel: | **=EX48!C27** |
| Lotus 1-2-3: | **+<<EX48>>C27** |

Copy this down to row 25 of the cash flow to pick up Product 2 direct costs, and then copy both through to November.

**Note:** There will normally be sales from January in the following year's budget that would be fed back to December.

## Cash flow timing assumption

Capital and overhead costs are paid for in the month shown in the budget, therefore, no offset is needed for them.

5 For capital costs (Vehicles), in B16 enter:

| | |
|---|---|
| Excel: | **=EX48!B15** |
| Lotus 1-2-3: | **+<<EX48>>B15** |

Copy down to row 17 to pick up capital costs (Machinery), and also to February and on through to December.

6 For overhead costs (accommodation), in B31 enter:

| | |
|---|---|
| Excel: | **=EX48!B33** |
| Lotus 1-2-3: | **+<<EX48>>B33** |

Copy down to rows 32 to 35 to pick up the rest of the overhead costs, and also to February and on through to December.

7 Add formulae for Total Cash in (Sum rows 8 to 9), Total Capital (sum rows 16 to 18), Total Direct Costs (Sum rows 24 to 26) and Total Cash out (row 19 + row 27+ row 37) from January through to December.

Now, if product volumes are changed in the sales forecast, the effect of them will be picked up, firstly by the budget forecast, and then by the cash flow forecast.

**Important:** Because the cash flow model is linked only to the budget model, the latter must be allowed to recalculate any changes in the sales forecast model so that the cash flow picks up the effect of the changes.

### Example 4.9 (★EX49)  The cash flow forecast

| | A | B | C | D | E | F | G | H | I |
|---|---|---|---|---|---|---|---|---|---|
| 1 | FILE : EX49.xls | | W I D G E T   M A K E R S   L T D | | | | | | |
| 2 | 6/12/1996 | | Cash Flow Forecast - 1997 | | | | | | |
| 3 | 4:24pm | | | | | | | | |
| 4 | | | | | | | | | |
| 5 | | Jan | Feb | Mar | Apr | May | Jun | Jul | Aug |
| 6 | CASH IN | | | | | | | | |
| 7 | (1 month after sale) | | | | | | | | |
| 8 | Cash in from sales | | 4250 | 4550 | 4874 | 5223 | 5601 | 6009 | 6450 |
| 9 | (Spare) | | | | | | | | |
| 10 | Total | 0 | 4250 | 4550 | 4874 | 5223 | 5601 | 6009 | 6450 |
| 11 | | | | | | | | | |
| 12 | CASH OUT | | | | | | | | |
| 13 | | | | | | | | | |
| 14 | CAPITAL COSTS | | | | | | | | |
| 15 | (Same month as cost) | | | | | | | | |
| 16 | Vehicles | 0 | 0 | 15000 | 0 | 0 | 0 | 0 | 0 |
| 17 | Machinery | 0 | 0 | 0 | 0 | 5000 | 0 | 0 | 0 |
| 18 | (Spare) | | | | | | | | |
| 19 | Total (A) | 0 | 0 | 15000 | 0 | 5000 | 0 | 0 | 0 |
| 20 | | | | | | | | | |
| 21 | | | | | | | | | |
| 22 | DIRECT COSTS | | | | | | | | |
| 23 | (1 month before sale) | | | | | | | | |
| 24 | Product 1 | 800 | 854 | 912 | 974 | 1041 | 1113 | 1191 | 1275 |
| 25 | Product 2 | 330 | 363 | 399 | 439 | 483 | 531 | 585 | 643 |
| 26 | (Spare) | | | | | | | | |
| 27 | Total (B) | 1130 | 1217 | 1311 | 1413 | 1524 | 1644 | 1775 | 1918 |
| 28 | | | | | | | | | |
| 29 | OVERHEADS | | | | | | | | |
| 30 | (Same month as cost) | | | | | | | | |
| 31 | Accommodation | 135 | 135 | 135 | 135 | 135 | 135 | 135 | 135 |
| 32 | Electricity | 120 | 120 | 120 | 120 | 120 | 120 | 120 | 120 |
| 33 | Gas | 68 | 68 | 68 | 68 | 68 | 68 | 68 | 68 |
| 34 | Telephone | 70 | 70 | 70 | 70 | 70. | 70 | 70 | 70 |
| 35 | Salaries | 3500 | 3500 | 3500 | 3500 | 3500 | 3500 | 3500 | 3500 |
| 36 | (Spare) | | | | | | | | |
| 37 | Total (C) | 3893 | 3893 | 3893 | 3893 | 3893 | 3893 | 3893 | 3893 |
| 38 | | | | | | | | | |
| 39 | TOTAL CASH OUT | | | | | | | | |
| 40 | ( A + B + C ) | | | | | | | | |
| 41 | Total (D) | 5023 | 5110 | 20204 | 5306 | 10417 | 5537 | 5668 | 5811 |

If all of the models are in memory at the same time this will occur automatically, otherwise the links may need to be 'refreshed'. The precise method of refreshing links varies between spreadsheets, and between versions of each type. In all cases, however, changes can be carried through by loading each into memory, in order of dependency. In this case the order would be *sales, budget, cash flow*.

# Examples of non-essential but useful techniques
■ ■ ■

Modern spreadsheets have so many facilities that it can be difficult for the newcomer to identify those that will be most useful for their particular application. As a general rule, applications are best kept as simple, and as small as possible, whilst achieving their objectives.

This section introduces some spreadsheet facilities and modelling techniques that are likely to be useful in budgeting and forecasting.

■ fixed column and row headings;

- percentages;
- averages;
- cumulative totals.

## Fixed column and row headings

Most spreadsheet models are larger than can be seen on the screen at normal 100 per cent view. More rows and columns can of course can be seen if the view is reduced to say 50 per cent, but then you may not be able to read it! The Window menu has two features to help – Split and Freeze Panes.

Place the cursor on the cell where you want a vertical and horizontal split, and as shown in Example 4.10 two windows appear. You can switch between them and move around in one window without affecting the column view in the other.

Now select Window, Freeze Panes – this 'freezes' the rows above and the columns to the left of the split position as shown in Example 4.11. Using this feature you can move anywhere on the spreadsheet and still be able to see your titles at the top and left.

70

### Example 4.10 (★EX410) Using 'Split' and 'Un-freeze'

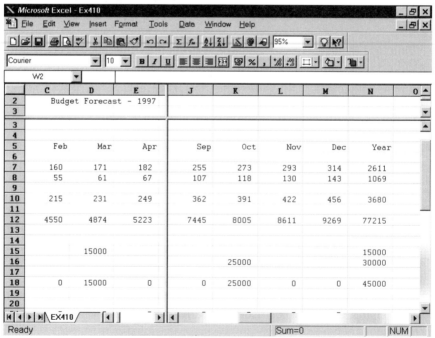

| | C | D | E | | J | K | L | M | N | O |
|---|---|---|---|---|---|---|---|---|---|---|
| 2 | Budget Forecast - 1997 | | | | | | | | | |
| 3 | | | | | | | | | | |
| 3 | | | | | | | | | | |
| 4 | | | | | | | | | | |
| 5 | Feb | Mar | Apr | | Sep | Oct | Nov | Dec | Year | |
| 6 | | | | | | | | | | |
| 7 | 160 | 171 | 182 | | 255 | 273 | 293 | 314 | 2611 | |
| 8 | 55 | 61 | 67 | | 107 | 118 | 130 | 143 | 1069 | |
| 9 | | | | | | | | | | |
| 10 | 215 | 231 | 249 | | 362 | 391 | 422 | 456 | 3680 | |
| 11 | | | | | | | | | | |
| 12 | 4550 | 4874 | 5223 | | 7445 | 8005 | 8611 | 9269 | 77215 | |
| 13 | | | | | | | | | | |
| 14 | | | | | | | | | | |
| 15 | | 15000 | | | | | | | 15000 | |
| 16 | | | | | | 25000 | | | 30000 | |
| 17 | | | | | | | | | | |
| 18 | 0 | 15000 | 0 | | 0 | 25000 | 0 | 0 | 45000 | |
| 19 | | | | | | | | | | |
| 20 | | | | | | | | | | |

## Example 4.11 (★EX411) Using 'split' and 'freeze panes'

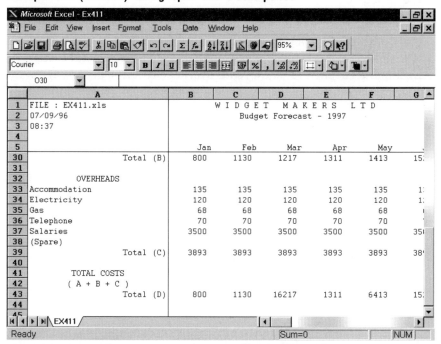

## Example 4.12 (★EX412) Using percentages on overhead costs

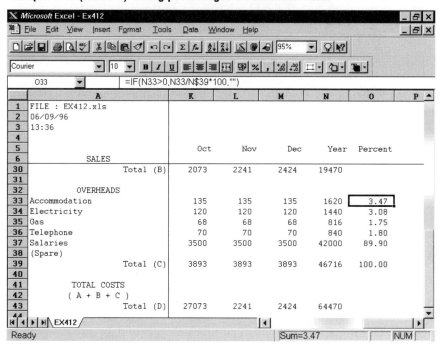

## Percentages

It can often be useful to show each item of a group of figures as a percentage of the total of a group. For instance, percentage of each overhead cost compared either, to total overheads, or to the grand total cost.

Example 4.12 (page 71) shows each overhead cost as a percentage of the total overhead cost.

## Averages

There are many reasons to use averages, and of course they can very easily be calculated using the SUM function; like this, for instance, on a set of six figures in C4 to C9:

**SUM(C4:C9)/6**

If, however, you want to exclude blank cells from the calculation, you can use the COUNT function in place of the divisor, like this:

**SUM(C4:C9)/COUNT(C4:C9)**

The *average* function also does the job of *sum/count*, like this:

**AVERAGE(C4:C9)**

Example 4.13 (below) illustrates each of these methods, and shows the way in which each handles a blank cell (b), or a zero value (c).

### Example 4.13 (★EX413) Averages calculated in different ways

|   | A | B | C | D | E | F | G | H |
|---|---|---|---|---|---|---|---|---|
| 1 | FILE : EX413.xls | | | | | | | |
| 2 | 3/10/96 | | (a) | (b) | (c) | | | |
| 3 | | | | | | | | |
| 4 | | | 1 | 1 | 1 | | | |
| 5 | | | 2 | 2 | 2 | | | |
| 6 | | | 3 | | 0 | | | |
| 7 | | | 4 | 4 | 4 | | | |
| 8 | | | 5 | 5 | 5 | | | |
| 9 | | | 6 | 6 | 6 | | | |
| 10 | | | | | | [ Formulae for column E ] | | |
| 11 | | | | | | | | |
| 12 | | SUM / 6 | 3.5 | 3 | 3 | = SUM(E4:E9)/6 | | |
| 13 | | | | | | | | |
| 14 | | SUM / COUNT | 3.5 | 3.6 | 3 | = SUM(E4:E9)/COUNT(E4:E9) | | |
| 15 | | | | | | | | |
| 16 | | AVERAGE FUNCTION | 3.5 | 3.6 | 3 | = AVG(E4:E9) | | |
| 17 | | | | | | | | |

## Cumulative totals

It can be very useful to be able to see at a glance the cumulative totals of each row to a given month, for instance, when comparing actual

## Example 4.14 (∗EX414)  Calculating cumulative totals

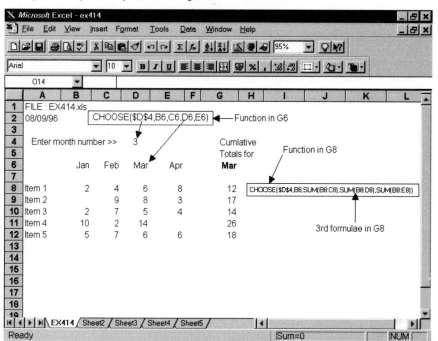

expenditure to date with that of the original budget. One way in which this can be done using the **CHOOSE** function is illustrated in Example 4.14.

To display the selected month – March in the example – the number of the month required (3 in this case) is entered in D4 and the CHOOSE function in G6 selects the third formulae, which simply repeats what is in D6 – 'Mar'.

To show cumulative totals in row 8 for example, the third function in G8 is SUM(B8..D8), which gives the cumulative total from January to March. Remember to make the location of the entered month number absolute – $D$4 – so that it doesn't change when copied down to rows 9–12.

## Summary

In this chapter, the principal spreadsheet techniques used for budgeting and forecasting have been explored.

■ Essential practices and conventions that will minimise errors and the likelihood of work being lost were noted:
- regular saving;
- backing up;
- version numbers;
- date and time stamps;
- cell protection;
- check sum;
- automatic recalculation.

■ Example sales, budget and cash flow forecast models were created, demonstrating many of the techniques that will be used later on, including file linking.

■ Additional non-essential, but useful techniques, were described and illustrated.

# PART 3

**■ ■ ■**

# A complete forecast from beginning to end

By extending the principles of budgeting in Part 1, and building on the spreadsheet essentials of Part 2, complete budget and cash flow forecasting models are created in Part 3.

Each stage is taken step by step, and as before, you will benefit most by constructing the stages yourself on a spreadsheet. The illustration disc already contains each of the completed stages.

The first task in the preparation of a budget is to decide what it will be used for.

# 5
∎ ∎ ∎

# Preparations for the budget

Review of the budgeting process ∎    77

The example business 'Widget Makers Ltd' ∎

Deciding the requirements of the example budget ∎

A single or departmental budget? ∎

Cost categories: definitions and examples ∎

Cost headings ∎

Categorising the cost headings ∎

Revenue headings ∎

The forecast's duration and periods ∎

# Review of the budgeting process
■ ■ ■

The key processes leading to allocation of a departmental budget within a larger company may include:

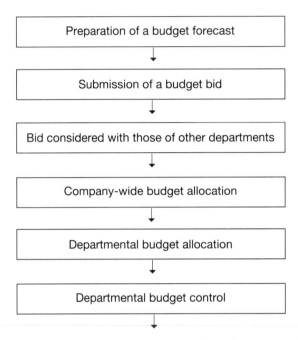

| Preparation of a budget forecast |
| --- |
| Submission of a budget bid |
| Bid considered with those of other departments |
| Company-wide budget allocation |
| Departmental budget allocation |
| Departmental budget control |

In a smaller company with no departmental breakdown, and where the budget is likely to be forecast, allocated and controlled by just a few managers, or perhaps only one, the process would simply be:

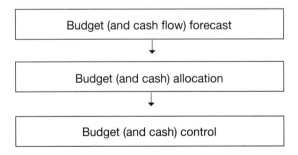

| Budget (and cash flow) forecast |
| --- |
| Budget (and cash) allocation |
| Budget (and cash) control |

It is more likely in this scenario that *cash flow control*, and hence *cash flow forecasting*, would be required.

It is the *budget* and *cash flow* forecasting part of the process that we are dealing with here.

# The example business 'Widget Makers Ltd'
■ ■ ■

To take in all aspects of budget forecasting, an example that requires a cash flow will be used (see Figure 5.1 below).

Widget Makers Ltd is owned by its managing director, who employs departmental senior managers for production, marketing and sales, and administration. There are 30 permanent non-management members of staff, and additional temporary staff are taken on for packing and distribution when sales volumes exceed the capacity of full-time personnel.

The company's business is making and selling two kinds of widgets. Widgets are specialist components used by other manufacturers.

The managing director personally prepares the budget *forecast* in liaison with, and input from, all of the department heads. She then gives each of them a budget *allocation*. Budget *control* is then maintained by the senior managers for their own departments, whilst the managing director retains overall visibility of cash flow, and ultimate budget control through regular monthly figures and reports from each of the departments.

### Figure 5.1 Widget Makers Ltd budgeting process

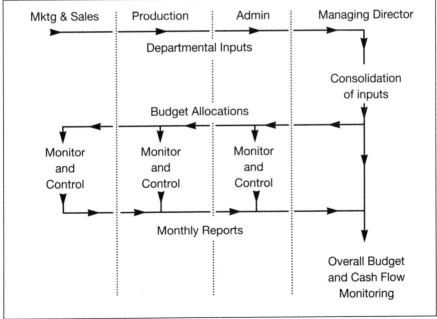

# Deciding the requirements of the example budget
■ ■ ■

The first task in the preparation of a budget is to decide what it will be used for. Chapter 2 explored some of the more common uses, which in summary were:

■ budget management;
■ planning and 'What-if';
■ cost control;
■ raising finance;
■ cash flow control.

Whilst it is, in theory, possible to devise one forecasting structure that will accommodate all of these requirements, in practice it is best to create discrete models for each, and link them as appropriate. It is, therefore, absolutely essential that a clear picture of precisely what is required from the budget is established before modelling starts.

We'll assume that the managing director and senior managers of Widget Makers Ltd decide that their budget forecast and allocation will be used for:

■ matching material and labour costs to sales forecasts;
■ forecasting budget requirements for each department;
■ forecasting cash requirements for the company overall;
■ allocating budgets to each department;
■ monitoring and controlling departmental budgets;
■ monitoring and controlling overall cash flow.

It is the facilities for these requirements that will be incorporated within the example budget.

# A single or departmental budget?
■ ■ ■

Should a budget be constructed as a single model for the whole company, embracing all of the departments, or should each department have its own forecast and allocation? As with most things, there is no absolute solution, but the answer usually depends principally upon:

■ the size and number of departments;
■ the degree of self-sufficiency versus interdependency of each department;

■ the extent to which the principal budget authority (the managing director in the case of Widget Makers Ltd) wishes to delegate forecasting and control.

> **Note:** whilst the technical way in which the spreadsheet models will be constructed and consolidated will of course depend upon the chosen method, there is no reason why either cannot be accommodated within the general objective of keeping things as simple as possible. Technical realisation should not therefore, in itself, be thought a constraint.

Considering each of these points for Widget Makers Ltd:

■ **Size and number of departments.** There are only three departments, and none of them very large.
■ **Self-sufficiency versus interdependency of each department.** There are only two products, widgets Mk1 and widgets Mk2, and, therefore, all of the departments are closely dependent one upon the other.
■ **Delegation of forecasting and control.** We have already seen that the managing director of Widget Makers Ltd prefers to prepare the budget forecast personally, in liaison with the senior managers, and to give each of them a budget allocation which they monitor and control. They provide the managing director with a budget report each month, and she monitors the overall budget and cash flow.

Thus, the options available to the managing director include:

1 Prepare three separate forecasts and allocations.

2 Prepare a single consolidated forecast, and provide three separate allocations.

3 Prepare a single consolidated forecast, and provide three allocations on a single model; that is, each senior manager sees all of the departmental allocations.

   Option 3 is probably best. Widget Makers Ltd is a small company with closely interrelated departments, and there is no reason why each department head should not be aware of the others' budget allocation – they have after all been involved in their preparation.

   Furthermore, because of the close departmental interrelation, any changes that will inevitably occur during the year, to the forecast levels

81

> **Cost categories are about what an item of expenditure is *for*, not what the item is. Thus each of two of the same item bought for different reasons may be in different cost categories.**

of widget sales, for instance, must therefore be communicated to all of the senior managers.

If all of the information is contained in a single model, not only is the task easier for the managing director who only has to update one spreadsheet, but the impact of the change on each of the departments can be seen by all of the senior managers who receive exactly the same information.

So Option 3 it is, and this is what will be used for the example.

# Cost categories: definitions and examples
■  ■  ■

## What cost categories are

Cost (or expense) categories are a means of identifying the various kinds of expenditure that are approached in different ways in a budget.

Much of what follows is guidance that should be interpreted according to the particular case or requirement. However, there are two rules that really must be adhered to:

### Rule 1: *Consistency of approach within a group of budgets*

If costs are not categorised consistently throughout a group of budgets, then it will be impossible to properly consolidate them for the whole company. It doesn't even matter if you completely ignore the guidance here and invent your own categories – so long as they do what is wanted, are understood by everyone involved, and are consistently applied.

### Rule 2: *Categorise according to use*

Cost categories are about what an item of expenditure is *for*, not what the item is. Thus each of two of the same item bought for different reasons may be in different cost categories.

The categories that will be discussed and used in the example are:

■  capital;
■  start up;
■  variable direct;

- constant direct;
- overhead.

The following sections define each of these categories, explain what they are for and provide typical examples. Where fairly common 'special cases' exist for a category, then they are also identified.

Also, bear in mind a general reason for separately identifying categories of cost – simply that of convenience for everyone who uses the budget.

Throughout the book, and especially in this section, the term 'product' should be taken to mean 'that which is sold to a customer'. The product may be a manufactured item, or a service; office cleaning, for instance, or simply advice – such as consultancy.

# Capital

## What?

Capital items are those that are not consumed by the product, and which have monetary value that could be realised by selling them. Capital items are sometimes known as *Fixed Assets*, the word 'fixed' referring to their non-consumable nature.

The value of most capital items will decrease with time and use, and the amount of value lost during a year is known as *Depreciation*. This is a figure more commonly encountered in a company's financial year end profit and loss statement and the balance sheet than in a budget, although of course the need to replace worn out or obsolete capital equipment must be considered in the budget, as capital expenditure!

## Why?

A budget forecast can be also be used as a simple profit and loss forecast (P&L), and capital expenditure will not usually figure in the calculation of profit. To be able to use the model as both a budget and a simple P&L it will be necessary to carry out calculations with and without capital expenditure.

## Examples

Any item that is not consumed, and which has a realisable monetary value, may be considered a capital item:

- buildings;
- plant and machinery;
- vehicles;
- higher value office equipment, such as a photocopiers and computers.

## Special Cases

In practice, most companies assign a minimum purchase price above which an item, or group of items, will be classified as capital. Thus, although the office kettle meets the criteria of possessing realisable value, and is not a consumable, it is unlikely to be classed as a capital item (the purchase of a kettle would be categorised as an overhead).

# Start up

## What?

Start up costs are those that occur only once because of the introduction of a new product, or indeed an entirely new business. Like capital items they are not consumables, but unlike capital items, they need not possess a realisable monetary value.

It is not important *when* the expense is incurred. Even six months after the start of the project, it will still be categorised as 'start up' if it is a 'once off' and exists only because of the new project.

## Why?

Start up costs, being one-off items of expenditure, will not usually be included in the calculations of ongoing profit or loss for a new product. Thus, in the same way as for capital items, if the budget is also to be used as a simple P&L forecast it will be necessary to exclude start up costs from the calculation.

## Examples

Any 'one-off' item of expenditure that occurs only because of a new product should be categorised as start up:

- tooling;
- setting up a production line;
- manufacturing drawings and specifications;
- updating sales literature.

## Special Cases

A start up cost may also be a capital item, such as an item of manufacturing equipment for a new product. In this case either category can be used, but it may be clearer to treat it as capital for the purpose of depreciation, because if depreciation is included in the budget it will extend beyond the budgeting period currently being considered.

# Variable direct

## What?

Variable direct costs are those that arise in the course of creating or providing a product. They are characterised principally by their rise and fall in sympathy with product volumes. Usually, if product volumes fall to zero, then so will variable direct costs.

Some businesses will have high variable direct costs, manufacturing, for example, will use raw materials or bought in parts. At the other extreme, if the product is advice or consultancy, then variable direct costs will be very low, or nonexistent.

## Why?

Because variable direct costs are wholly related to product volumes, it is vitally important that they are clearly identified and linked to forecast levels of business. The greater the proportion of variable direct costs to the total cost, the greater their significance and impact.

85

## Examples

Any cost that varies according to product volumes should be categorised as a variable direct:

■ raw materials and parts for manufacturing;

■ vehicle fuel for a delivery service;

■ labour costs paid only for work done;

■ items bought in for resale.

## Special Cases

There will sometimes be costs that are either only loosely related to product volumes, or, are so small that they are more suitably categorised in another way.

For example, the cost of sales invoice forms is likely to vary with product volumes, but, their total cost – in any event – is so small compared to the total costs of the company that, they are best categorised as an overhead.

Another example – in the case of a self-employed consultant who is visited at his office by clients, there are no additional costs, worthy of note, created by more customers walking through the door. Thus, the consultant has no variable direct costs.

# Constant direct

## What?

These are also costs that exist only because the product exists, but they are not influenced by sales volumes as quickly, or, to the same extent, as the direct variables. Whereas direct variable costs become zero immediately product volumes cease, constant directs are more likely to continue for days, weeks, or even months after production ceases.

Constant direct costs generally represent the ongoing investment in plant and manpower necessary for a given product.

## Why?

It is important, especially in a business with more than one product, to be able to measure the profitability of each product or range of products. Identifying the direct constant costs, together with the direct variables, enables the total direct costs associated with the product to be calculated.

**Gross profit is calculated by sales value – total direct costs.**

## Examples

Costs that exist only because of the product, but which are not immediately and extensively affected by changes in product volumes, should be categorised as constant directs:

- routine maintenance of product-specific plant and machinery;
- full-time product-specific personnel;
- heating and lighting of product-specific areas;
- after-sales customer service.

## Special Cases

Sometimes the difference between constant direct costs and overheads may not be readily apparent, and in the case of a small, single-product company, they are probably one and the same. In either case categorising the cost as an overhead will usually be the best solution.

# Overhead

## What?

Overheads are costs not related to any particular product, and which are not expended on capital or start up items. In other words, everything not included in one of the other categories.

This does *not* mean that the overhead category is in any way a general dustbin, or, somewhere to put items rather than properly consider how they should be categorised.

The point about the term 'overhead' is that it means 'over and above' the direct costs of a product. Overheads are sometimes known as indirect costs.

## Why?

Overheads are the final figures to complete the calculation of the total cost of running the business.

**Net profit is calculated by sales value – direct costs + overheads.**

## Examples

Any cost not related to a particular product may be categorised as an overhead:

- rent;
- telephone;
- general administration;
- office heating and lighting.

## Special Cases

Whilst most companies employing more than a handful of personnel will be able to clearly identify overheads, in any business that has just one product it will probably not be possible to separate constant direct and overhead costs. Looking at it another way – if product volumes in a single-product, one-man business fall to zero, then for all practical purposes the business no longer exists! Thus, in these cases, any distinction between constant direct and overhead costs is immaterial.

These then are the cost categories that will be used for the example budget

*Remember: Categorise costs according to what they are for, not what they are.*

# Cost headings

■ ■ ■

Having identified the cost categories, we now need to consider the individual headings within them. This is principally a matter of deciding how much to separate the costs, and how much to group them together, whilst ensuring that every cost of the business is accounted for.

The extremes available are:

■ group all costs as a single heading within their category;

■ assign an individual heading to every conceivable item of expenditure, such as 'paper clips', 'light bulbs', 'nuts', 'bolts', and so on.

Clearly, whilst both extremes achieve the objective of accounting for every cost of the business, neither one of them is satisfactory. Grouping all costs within each category obscures most of the important details, and separating every possible cost provides far too many, and would certainly be quite impracticable.

The answer is to consider what is needed in the context of the required objectives of the budget – match the cost headings to them, whilst providing sufficient detail for the purpose – yet not so much that the wood can't be seen for the trees.

However, there is a single factor that, when considered, will in most cases determine the cost headings for you. This most important element is:

**An ability to compare actual figures with the forecast.**

Why is this so basic? It is because there is a fundamental truth of all forecasts – they are wrong! Or, perhaps more generously, they are rarely absolutely right, and the forecaster's job is to continuously review and refine the forecasts to make them as accurate as possible. The way to check the accuracy of a forecast is to compare actual figures with it as they become available (taking in actual figures and reviewing forecasts is dealt with in Chapter 9).

Now, this may seem rather too obvious to dwell upon, but, in fact, it is a very common mistake indeed. All too often forecasts are broken down into headings that are both difficult and impractical to check against actual data. Thus, in deciding cost headings, it is essential to first consider what actual figures will be available each month, and ensure that their collection is a practicable proposition.

# Obtaining actual figures for comparison

The way in which actual data can be collected depends very much upon the company's size and the organisation of its book-keeping. Here it is necessary, for the first and last time, to look briefly at one aspect of the way in which the books work.

There is a book known as the *nominal ledger* (nowadays this 'book' is more likely to be on a computer, but its purpose and principle is identical to that of a manual system). The only things about the nominal ledger that we need be aware of are that it contains a record of every transaction, both in and out of the business, and that each of the transactions is allocated to a nominal code. Thus, it is the ideal source of actual figures.

> There is a book known as the *nominal ledger* (nowadays this 'book' is more likely to be on a computer, but its purpose and principle is identical to that of a manual system). The only things about the nominal ledger that we need be aware of are that it contains a record of every transaction, both in and out of the business, and that each of the transactions is allocated to a nominal code.

The nominal codes, or N/C's, are often simply a set of numbers that are structured in a way that matches the categories we discussed earlier. An example will help:

| Nominal codes | Category of cost or revenue |
|---|---|
| 0100 – 0150 | Capital expenditure |
| 0200 – 0300 | Direct variable costs |
| 0350 – 0400 | Constant direct costs |
| 0450 – 0600 | Overheads |
| 0800 – 0825 | Sales Widgets Mk1 |
| 0850 – 0875 | Sales Widgets Mk2 |

and so on ...

The individual numbers within the ranges shown are then allocated to each chosen item of cost or revenue. Taking the overheads category, for example, nominal codes 0450 through to 0600 are available for allocation to whatever costs are wanted, perhaps like this:

| Nominal code | Item of cost |
|---|---|
| 0450 | Rent |
| 0451 | Rates |
| 0452 | Electricity |
| 0453 | Gas |

and so on ...

**Note:** The way in which nominal codes are grouped or structured is not random, and will probably have a significant bearing on the way in which the company's audited *profit and loss statement* and *balance sheet* are produced at the end of its financial year. Designing a nominal ledger structure is therefore best done in co-operation with the company's accountant or auditors.

So, now we can see that the cost headings needed in the budget are nothing more or less than those used for the nominal ledger. They should meet all of the required criteria – their number and structure will almost certainly be appropriate, and most importantly, because the nominal ledger contains all of the company's transactions, it is a very simple matter to obtain from it the actual figures that are required each month.

Also, if the budget is likely to be used in conjunction with the company's year end accounts, it is very well worthwhile first looking at these and considering all of the headings in the profit and loss and balance sheet statements.

Now, whilst using the nominal ledger as the source of actual figures is easily achieved in a company that is not so large that everyone who needs it has access to the books, it won't necessarily be as straightforward for a single department of a larger company.

In corporate situations there may be a devolved system of nominal codes, such that each department keeps only those figures appropriate to it, and forwards the actuals to a central point each month where they are consolidated with those from other departments. This is fine – the department can also use these actual figures for reviewing its forecast.

Alternatively, there may be a policy of all financial transactions being handled by the central point; in which case the central point will be responsible for passing back actual figures to each department so that they can review their own forecasts. For this system to work in a way that will be useful to departmental managers, the actual figures must be passed back to them very soon after the end of each financial period.

The ability of departmental managers to take effective action based on actual financial performance is inversely proportional to the time it takes to get the figures to them.

Finally, it may be that a department has no access whatever to the company's nominal ledger figures, or that these are structured in a way that is of no practical use to it. In such cases, there is no reason to stop a department from inventing its own system of cost and revenue headings. It can in effect design a 'nominal code' structure for its own exclusive use. This will work quite satisfactorily so long as the basic rules concerning the number of headings, and especially the availability of actual data for comparison purposes, are properly observed.

## Choosing cost headings for the example budget

In a new business of course, the needs of both the nominal ledger and the budget forecasts can be taken into account when the nominal structure is designed. For the purpose of Widget Makers Ltd, we'll simply choose a representative selection of cost (and later on revenue headings) as follows:

### Widget Makers Ltd cost headings in alphabetical order

- Building maintenance
- Design of Widget Mk3
- Diesel fuel (Deliveries)
- Electricity
- Gas
- Machine maintenance (Factory)
- Machine maintenance (Office)
- Machinery (Factory capital)
- Machinery (Office capital)
- Parts for Widgets Mk1
- Parts for Widgets Mk2
- Petrol (Manager's cars)
- Postage
- Rates
- Rent
- Salaries (Management)
- Salaries (Widget production)
- Stationery
- Telephone
- Vehicle maintenance (Delivery)
- Vehicle maintenance (Managers)
- Wages (Temporary staff)

This is not intended to be an exhaustive list, but is designed to illustrate the use of cost categories in the example budget.

# Categorising the cost headings
■ ■ ■

Having established which cost headings will be used, it is now only necessary to allocate them to the appropriate categories. One way of doing this is to take each of the categories in turn, and select the appropriate headings for each.

## Capital

Any item that is not consumed, and which has a realisable monetary value:

- Machinery (Factory capital)
- Machinery (Office capital)

## Start up

Any 'one-off' item of expenditure that occurs only because of a new product:

- Design of Widget Mk3

## Variable direct

Any costs that vary according to product volumes:

- Diesel fuel (Deliveries)
- Parts for Widgets Mk1
- Parts for Widgets Mk2
- Wages (Temporary staff)

## Constant direct

Costs that exist only because of the product, but which are not immediately and extensively affected by changes in product volumes:

- Electricity
- Gas
- Machine maintenance (Factory)
- Salaries (Widget production)
- Vehicle maintenance (Delivery)

> **Note:** Although the office space uses electricity and gas for lighting and heating, the amount is insignificant compared to that consumed by the factory. Furthermore, if production ceased altogether, the factory costs of electricity and gas would be gone. Thus, *constant direct* is more appropriate for these costs than *overheads*.

## Overhead

Any cost not related to a particular product:

- Building maintenance

- Machine maintenance (Office)
- Petrol (Manager's cars)
- Postage
- Rates
- Rent
- Salaries (Management)
- Stationery
- Telephone
- Vehicle maintenance (Managers)

**Note:** Although the factory occupies far more space than the offices, the building and its associated costs of maintenance, rates and rent are an integral part of the whole business, and they would still exist even if production stopped altogether. Thus *overheads* are more appropriate than *constant direct* for these costs.

# Revenue headings

■  ■  ■

Revenue headings are selected on exactly the same principle as those for cost headings. The nominal ledger is the first place to look for guidance, the number of headings should be appropriate to the need, and of course, an ability to compare actual performance with the forecast is of paramount importance.

If a budget is driven by sales volumes, as the example budget will be, then the revenue headings should be aligned with them. Thus, if there are two product's sales volumes in the budget, then there must be two matching revenue headings. And exactly the same rationale applies if one of the requirements of the model is to assess the individual profitability of products – matched cost and revenue headings are needed.

In the case of Widget Makers Ltd, there will be two product's sales volumes driving the budget – Widgets Mk1 and Widgets Mk2 – and so, two matching revenue headings are needed.

### Widget Makers Ltd revenue headings

- Widgets Mk1
- Widgets Mk2

# The forecast's duration and periods

■  ■  ■

## Duration and starting point

A budget forecast can be made for any duration, although one year is most commonly used.

For long-term business planning several years may be required, and this can be achieved either by creating a single model of the required duration, say five years, or by building five separate, but linked, one-year models. In almost every case, the latter is preferable for the sake of size and manageability. The trick is to concentrate entirely on the first year until you are sure that the model meets your needs, then simply make four more copies, which only takes a few seconds, amend their titles, link the end of each year to the start of the next, and there are you are – a five-year business plan.

For Widget Makers Ltd we'll create a one-year forecast.

Again, the forecast can start at any point in the calendar that is required. It is best, however, to align the forecast with the company's financial year, whatever that may be – from 1 January to 31 December for instance, or perhaps 1st April to 31 March to line up with the Inland Revenue's financial year.

Widget Makers Ltd start their financial year on 1 January.

## The number of periods

Within the span of a forecast, any number of periods can be used. However, the number of periods, just like the cost and revenue headings, must be aligned with the way in which actual figures are obtained.

Quite simply, if, for example, the nominal ledger uses 12 calendar monthly periods in a year, then the budget's periods must be aligned with them. Some companies prefer to use 13 fixed periods of four weeks, because they find this better suited to their requirements.

In a minority of cases, 52 or 53 one-week periods are used where a longer period would obscure high impact but short-term influences. For example, where rapid cash flows are likely to overstretch the company's borrowing facilities with their bank. In the case of weekly forecasts, actual figures can be obtained four weekly for comparison, either by setting up a dual system that is linked to the weekly forecast, but which is expressed in four weekly blocks, or by converting the four weekly actual figures back to one weekly values. However, it is not advisable, although it is of course possible, to do this with calendar monthly periods, because of the irregular and fractional number of weeks there are in the months of the year (a decimalised calendar would make things so much easier for professional forecasters!).

## Summary

In this chapter all of the preparatory work for creating a budget forecast has been done.

■ The example business Widget Makers Ltd and its budgeting process have been defined. The managing director personally creates the forecasts in liaison with the departmental heads.

■ The objectives and requirements of the budget forecast have been defined:

■ matching material and labour costs to sales forecasts;

■ forecasting budget requirements for each department;

■ forecasting cash requirements for the company overall;

■ allocating budgets to each department;

■ monitoring and controlling departmental budgets;

■ monitoring and controlling overall cash flow.

■ A single budget model that everyone will use was decided, rather than an individual one for each department.

■ Cost and revenue categories were explained, and examples given.

■ It was shown that the nominal ledger is the first place to look for a list of cost and revenue headings, because that is likely to be the source of actual figures when reviewing the forecast. However, there are other ways of achieving this if the nominal ledger is inappropriate for any reason.

■ The cost headings chosen for Widget Makers Ltd were assigned to their categories.

■ Forecast duration and periods were discussed, a one-year span with 12 calendar monthly periods was decided for Widget Makers Ltd.

There are quite a few steps in building the budget forecast, and they can look a little daunting when described in full detail, as they will be here. Similarly , if all of the formulae for the model were shown in an illustration, they too might seem much more involved and complex than they really are.

# 6

$\blacksquare$ $\blacksquare$ $\blacksquare$

# Creating the budget framework

The sales forecast $\blacksquare$

The budget forecast $\blacksquare$

The cash flow forecast $\blacksquare$

In this chapter only the basic frameworks will be built. Additional facilities will be added in Part 4, as they are needed, when the practical use of the forecasts is examined in more detail.

> **Important:** Although each of the forecast models are complete, and all are fully described, the steps to completion will be very much eas-

# The sales forecast
■ ■ ■

The sales forecast is in effect already built, the one we created in Chapter 4 as Example 4.6 (★**EX46**) is what is required, with only minor changes to some row titles, and of course to the figures.

> All of the steps described below have been completed for ★ **SALES01** on the illustration disc.

### Steps for creating the sales forecast:

1  The first job is to make a copy of Example 4.6 (★**EX46**). If you have created it yourself, then of course you may have used a different file name. Give the copy the file name SALES01.

2  An easy and foolproof way of making a copy with a new file name:

   **a**  Load the file of which a copy is required.

   **b**  Use 'Save As' and *change the file name to the new one required*.

   **c**  Then *immediately* amend the file name in cell A1 and save again. This time the 'save' process will automatically assign the file name used in step b.

3  Now change all of the row titles that are 'Product 1' and 'Product 2', to 'Widgets Mk1' and 'Widgets Mk2' respectively.

4  Leave the figures that already exist as they are. Although they will be changed in due course, they will do for now to test the system as it is created (if you have already taken them out – put them back!).

**Example 6.1 (★SALES01)  The completed framework for the sales forecast**

| | A | B | C | D | E | F | G | |
|---|---|---|---|---|---|---|---|---|
| 1 | FILE : SALES01.xls | | W I D G E T | M A K E R S | L T D | | | |
| 2 | 06/09/96 | | | Sales Forecast 1997 | | | | |
| 3 | 14:56 | | | | | | | |
| 4 | *** SALES *** | Jan | Feb | Mar | Apr | May | Jun | |
| 5 | Volume | | | | | | | |
| 6 | Widgets Mk1 | 100 | 105 | 110 | 116 | 122 | 128 | |
| 7 | Widgets Mk2 | 50 | 55 | 61 | 67 | 73 | 81 | |
| 8 | (Spare) | | | | | | | |
| 9 | Total Volume | 150 | 160 | 171 | 182 | 195 | 208 | |
| 10 | | | | | | | | |
| 11 | Price (£) | | | | | | | |
| 12 | Widgets Mk1 | 25 | 25 | 25 | 25 | 25 | 25 | |
| 13 | Widgets Mk2 | 35 | 35 | 35 | 35 | 35 | 35 | |
| 14 | | | | | | | | |
| 15 | Sales Value (£) | | | | | | | |
| 16 | Widgets Mk1 | 2500 | 2625 | 2756 | 2894 | 3039 | 3191 | |
| 17 | Widgets Mk2 | 1750 | 1925 | 2118 | 2329 | 2562 | 2818 | |
| 18 | (Spare) | | | | | | | |
| 19 | Total Value | 4250 | 4550 | 4874 | 5223 | 5601 | 6009 | |

99

And that's it, until the proper sales volume figures and prices are entered.

# The budget forecast
■ ■ ■

There are quite a few steps in building the budget forecast, and they can look a little daunting when described in full detail, as they will be here. Similarly, if all of the formulae for the model were shown in an illustration, they too might seem much more involved and complex than they really are.

An important fact to bear in mind is that the formulae, in most of the 'months' columns, are simply copies automatically generated using the spreadsheet's copying facility. For this reason, the illustrations in the book show only columns that include unique formulae. It is, therefore, important to look carefully at the column labels – A, B, etc – and their headings below them.

As a further aid to clarity, the budget forecast is illustrated in two ways, firstly, as it will look in normal use, and secondly, displaying the contents of the cells so that the formulae can be seen. In the latter case, columns for the illustration have been widened so that they can accommodate the longer formulae. Figure 6.2 (opposite) shows what the budget forecast will look like in normal use when the steps described have been completed. Months February to December are not shown.

## Steps for creating the budget forecast

> All of the steps described below have been completed for ★**BUDG01** on the illustration disc.

You will probably find it helpful to refer to the formulae display in Figure 6.3 (see page 104) occasionally.

1  The basic structure of Example 4.8 (★**EX48**) provides a good start to the budget model, so make a copy of it as file name BUDG01

2  Change the row titles as shown in Figure 6.2, inserting new rows as required. When inserting rows in existing blocks, for example 'OVER-HEADS', place the cursor on 'Spare', or above it, so that the existing SUM calculation for the block remains valid.

3  Enter SUM formulae for the 'Total' rows of the new blocks in column B, for example 'START UP – Total (B)' is **SUM(B24:B25)**, and copy them all across to column M (December).

4  Enter formulae for the variable direct costs 'diesel fuel' and 'wages' in column B. Both of these are related to 'total sales volume', and so the formulae are **B10*B31** and **B10*B32** respectively. Copy both across to column M (December)

> **Note:** I actually used **B$10*B31** for 'diesel fuel', and then copied that formulae to all of the cells for it and 'wages' in one operation, the $ sign fixed the first part of the formulae to row 10.

5  The file link formulae for 'sales volume' and 'value' need to be changed, because if you are using a copy of ★**EX48** they will still refer to file ★**EX46**. Also, the link formulae for the new rows in the 'SALES' block

## Figure 6.2 (★BUDG01 – Normal display)
## The completed framework for the budget forecast

```
|          A           || B ||  N  ||  O  ||  P  |
 1    FILE : BUDG01.xls
 2       19/10/1996
 3       10:13pm
 4
 5                               Jan     Year           Check
 6                 SALES                                Sums
 7    Volume - Widgets Mk1        100     2611
 8    Volume - Widgets Mk2         50     1069
 9    (Spare)
10              Total volume      150     3680
11
12    Value - Widgets Mk1        2500    39793
13    Value - Widgets Mk2        1750    37422
14    (Spare)
15             Total £ Value     4250    77215
16    - - - - - - - - - - - - - - - - - - - - - - - - - - - - - -
17          CAPITAL COSTS
18    Factory machinery                 15000
19    Office machinery                  30000
20    (Spare)
21                  Total (A)      0     45000           45000
22    - - - - - - - - - - - - - - - - - - - - - - - - - - - - - -
23          START UP COSTS
24    Design of Widget Mk3
25    (Spare)
26                  Total (B)      0                         0
27    - - - - - - - - - - - - - - - - - - - - - - - - - - - - - -
28    VARIABLE DIRECT COSTS / ITEM
29    Parts for Widgets Mk1         5
30    Parts for Widgets Mk2         6
31    Diesel fuel (Deliveries)
32    Wages (Temporary staff)
33    (Spare)
34
35        VARIABLE DIRECT COSTS
36          (Vol x Cost / Item)
37    Parts for Widgets Mk1       500    13055
38    Parts for Widgets Mk2       300     6415
39    Diesel fuel (Deliveries)     0
40    Wages (Temporary staff)      0
41    (Spare)
42                  Total (C)    800     19470           19470
43    - - - - - - - - - - - - - - - - - - - - - - - - - - - - - -
44        CONSTANT DIRECT COSTS
45    Electricity
46    Gas
47    Machine maintenance (Factory)
48    Salaries (Widget production)
49    Vehicle maintenance (Delivery)
50    (Spare)
51                  Total (D)      0                         0
52    - - - - - - - - - - - - - - - - - - - - - - - - - - - - - -
53            OVERHEADS
54    Building maintenance
55    Machine maintenance (Office)
56    Petrol (Manager's cars)
57    Postage
58    Rates
59    Salaries (Management)
60    Stationery
61    Telephone
62    Vehicle maintenance (Managers)
63    (Spare)
64                  Total (E)      0                         0
65    - - - - - - - - - - - - - - - - - - - - - - - - - - - - - -
66          TOTAL COSTS
67          ( A+B+C+D+E )
68                  Total (F)    800     64470           64470
69    ================================================================
```

need to be entered. The link formulae in column B for the 'SALES' block should be:

| Row heading | Link formulae | |
|---|---|---|
| | *Excel* | *Lotus 1-2-3* |
| Volume – Widgets Mk1 | =**SALES01!B6** | +<<**SALES01**>>**B6** |
| Volume – Widgets Mk2 | =**SALES01!B7** | +<<**SALES01**>>**B7** |
| Value – Widgets Mk1 | =**SALES01!B16** | +<<**SALES01**>>**B16** |
| Value – Widgets Mk2 | =**SALES01!B17** | +<<**SALES01**>>**B17** |

Now copy these across to column M (December).

6  The 'total costs' SUM formulae at the bottom needs to be amended, in column B it should now be:

Total costs      **B21 + B26 + B42 + B51 + B64**

and copy this across to column M (December).

7  In the 'year total' column N, there will now be gaps in the formulae
that total each row for the year. Use any of the existing column N formulae to copy to wherever it is needed. (It is *not* needed, for example, for the 'variable direct costs/item' block, these are rates, and annual figures for them would be meaningless.)

> **Note:** The year SUM formulae shown prevent zero appearing if there are no figures in a row. If that facility is not required the formulae can be replaced by a simple SUM formulae, such as **SUM(B7:M7)** for row 7.

8  Error detecting check sums are needed. There are many ways to perform a check sum, of course. In this case I have chosen to have a separate check for each of the costs category blocks, and then add all of them together for comparison with the full year total costs. I have then put a check sum warning flag near the top left of the spreadsheet where it is most likely to be seen. The steps for the check sum are:

Create a named range that embraces all of the cells for each of the cost category blocks, for example, the range for 'Constant direct costs' is B45:M50 The ranges and names given to them in ★**BUDG01** are:

| Cost Category block | Range | Name of created range |
|---|---|---|
| CAPITAL | B18:M20 | Capital |
| START UP COSTS | B24:M25 | Startup |
| VARIABLE DIRECT COSTS | B37:M41 | Variable |
| CONSTANT DIRECT COSTS | B45:M50 | Constant |
| OVERHEADS | B54:M63 | Overheads |

Enter a SUM formulae for each of the ranges, in column P, as follows:

| In cell | Enter |
|---|---|
| P21 | SUM(CAPITAL) |
| P26 | SUM(STARTUP) |
| P42 | SUM(VARIABLE) |
| P51 | SUM(CONSTANT) |
| P64 | SUM(OVERHEADS) |

We now need to add up all of these SUM's, I have done it by creating yet another named range 'Checkout', which is P6:P64, and putting **SUM(CHECKOUT)** in P68. This calculation should be the same as the year total costs in N68.

Finally, it is useful to have a warning message appear somewhere easily seen if the two totals are not the same. I have put it in A4, using the formulae:

**IF(INT(SUM(CHECKOUT))<>INT(N68),"!!!! CHECK SUM ERROR !!!!","")**

Thus, A4 will be blank if everything adds up properly, or, will display the message if not.

All the formulae described are in Figure 6.3 (see page 104).

That completes work on the budget forecast framework until real values are entered later on.

103

# The cash flow forecast
■ ■ ■

A cash flow forecast is not always essential, and they are less likely to be used the further the controller of the budget is from the controller of the company's cash flow – the person who actually sends out sales invoices and makes payments. But, of course, before the advent of computers in business, it was difficult enough for even one person to fully understand the cash flow.

Nowadays, however, it really is very easy indeed for budget controllers to understand and keep track of the cash flow generated by their budget. And by doing so, they will be making their contribution to the company's overall cash resources. Consider the impact of say ten departments in a middle size company improving cash flow by just 5 per cent each.

**Note:** Because some users will not be concerned with VAT, although it is a very important aspect for those who are, it will be added into the cash flow forecast only after the whole system is complete in all other respects.

Back to Widget Makers Ltd, however, who most certainly do need to monitor and control their cash.

In the same way as for the budget, the cash flow forecast illustrations are presented in both 'normal' and 'formulae' display formats.

Figure 6.4 (see opposite) shows how the finished framework will look. Note that months March to December have been hidden for the sake of clarity.

## Figure 6.3 (★BUDG01 – Formulae display)
## The formulae in the budget forecast

```
          |        A         ||        B        ||              N              ||    O    ||   P   ||
 1   FILE : BUDG01.xls
 2   = NOW ()
 3   = TIME VALUE (A2)
 4   IF(INT(SUM(CHECKOUT))<>INT(N68),"!!!! CHECK SUM ERROR !!!!","")
 5                                       Jan                      Year                            Check
 6          SALES                                                                                 Sums
 7   Volume - Widgets Mk1           SALES01!B6       IF(SUM(B7:M7)<>0,SUM(B7:M7),"")
 8   Volume - Widgets Mk2           SALES01!B7       IF(SUM(B8:M8)<>0,SUM(B8:M8),"")
 9   (Spare)                                         IF(SUM(B9:M9)<>0,SUM(B9:M9),"")
10              Total volume SUM(B7:B9)              IF(SUM(B10:M10)<>0,SUM(B10:M10),"")
11
12   Value - Widgets Mk1            SALES01!B16      IF(SUM(B12:M12)<>0,SUM(B12:M12),"")
13   Value - Widgets Mk2            SALES01!B17      IF(SUM(B13:M13)<>0,SUM(B13:M13),"")
14   (Spare)
15              Total £ Value SUM(B12:B14)          IF(SUM(B15:M15)<>0,SUM(B15:M15),"")
16   --------------------------------------------------------------------------------------------------------
17          CAPITAL COSTS                           IF(SUM(B17:M17)<>0,SUM(B17:M17),"")
18   Factory machinery                              IF(SUM(B18:M18)<>0,SUM(B18:M18),"")
19   Office machinery                               IF(SUM(B19:M19)<>0,SUM(B19:M19),"")
20   (Spare)                                        IF(SUM(B20:M20)<>0,SUM(B20:M20),"")
21              Total (A) SUM(B18:B20)              IF(SUM(B21:M21)<>0,SUM(B21:M21),"")   SUM(CAPITAL)
22   --------------------------------------------------------------------------------------------------------
23          START UP COSTS
24   Design of Widget Mk3                           IF(SUM(B24:M24)<>0,SUM(B24:M24),"")
25   (Spare)                                        IF(SUM(B25:M25)<>0,SUM(B25:M25),"")
26              Total (B) SUM(B24:B25)              IF(SUM(B26:M26)<>0,SUM(B26:M26),"")   SUM(STARTUP)
27   --------------------------------------------------------------------------------------------------------
28   VARIABLE DIRECT COSTS / ITEM                   IF(SUM(B28:M28)<>0,SUM(B28:M28),"")
29   Parts for Widgets Mk1          5
30   Parts for Widgets Mk2          6
31   Diesel fuel (Deliveries)
32   Wages (Temporary staff)
33   (Spare)
34                                                  IF(SUM(B34:M34)<>0,SUM(B34:M34),"")
35       VARIABLE DIRECT COSTS                      IF(SUM(B35:M35)<>0,SUM(B35:M35),"")
36       (Vol x Cost / Item)                        IF(SUM(B36:M36)<>0,SUM(B36:M36),"")
37   Parts for Widgets Mk1          B7*B29          IF(SUM(B37:M37)<>0,SUM(B37:M37),"")
38   Parts for Widgets Mk2          B8*B30          IF(SUM(B38:M38)<>0,SUM(B38:M38),"")
39   Diesel fuel (Deliveries)       B$10*B31        IF(SUM(B39:M39)<>0,SUM(B39:M39),"")
40   Wages (Temporary staff)        B$10*B32        IF(SUM(B40:M40)<>0,SUM(B40:M40),"")
41   (Spare)                                        IF(SUM(B41:M41)<>0,SUM(B41:M41),"")
42              Total (C) SUM(B37:B41)              IF(SUM(B42:M42)<>0,SUM(B42:M42),"")   SUM(VARIABLE)
43   --------------------------------------------------------------------------------------------------------
44          CONSTANT DIRECT COSTS
45   Electricity                                    IF(SUM(B45:M45)<>0,SUM(B45:M45),"")
46   Gas                                            IF(SUM(B46:M46)<>0,SUM(B46:M46),"")
47   Machine maintenance (Factory)                  IF(SUM(B47:M47)<>0,SUM(B47:M47),"")
48   Salaries (Widget production)                   IF(SUM(B48:M48)<>0,SUM(B48:M48),"")
49   Vehicle maintenance (Delivery)                 IF(SUM(B49:M49)<>0,SUM(B49:M49),"")
50   (Spare)                                        IF(SUM(B50:M50)<>0,SUM(B50:M50),"")
51              Total (D) SUM(B45:B50)              IF(SUM(B51:M51)<>0,SUM(B51:M51),"")   SUM(CONSTANT)
52   --------------------------------------------------------------------------------------------------------
53          OVERHEADS                               IF(SUM(B53:M53)<>0,SUM(B53:M53),"")
54   Building maintenance                           IF(SUM(B54:M54)<>0,SUM(B54:M54),"")
55   Machine maintenance (Office)                   IF(SUM(B55:M55)<>0,SUM(B55:M55),"")
56   Petrol (Manager's cars)                        IF(SUM(B56:M56)<>0,SUM(B56:M56),"")
57   Postage                                        IF(SUM(B57:M57)<>0,SUM(B57:M57),"")
58   Rates                                          IF(SUM(B58:M58)<>0,SUM(B58:M58),"")
59   Salaries (Management)                          IF(SUM(B59:M59)<>0,SUM(B59:M59),"")
60   Stationery                                     IF(SUM(B60:M60)<>0,SUM(B60:M60),"")
61   Telephone                                      IF(SUM(B61:M61)<>0,SUM(B61:M61),"")
62   Vehicle maintenance (Managers)                 IF(SUM(B62:M62)<>0,SUM(B62:M62),"")
63   (Spare)                                        IF(SUM(B63:M63)<>0,SUM(B63:M63),"")
64              Total (E) SUM(B54:B63)              IF(SUM(B64:M64)<>0,SUM(B64:M64),"")   SUM(OVERHEADS)
65   --------------------------------------------------------------------------------------------------------
66          TOTAL COSTS                             IF(SUM(B66:M66)<>0,SUM(B66:M66),"")
67        ( A+B+C+D+E )                             IF(SUM(B67:M67)<>0,SUM(B67:M67),"")
68              Total (F) B21+B26+B42+B51+B64       IF(SUM(B68:M68)<>0,SUM(B68:M68),"")   SUM(CHECKOUT)
69   ========================================================================================================
```

## Figure 6.4 (*CASH01 – Normal display)
## The completed framework for the cash flow forecast

```
              |        A        ||  B  ||  C  ||  N  ||  O  ||  P  |
  1    FILE : CASH01.xls                 W I D G E T   M A K E R S   L T D
  2    20/10/1996                        Cash Flow Forecast - 1997
  3    5:17pm
  4
  5                                    Jan    Feb    Year          Check
  6              CASH IN                                           Sums
  7    From sales - Widgets Mk1          2500   35517
  8    From sales - Widgets Mk2          1750   32430
  9    (Spare)
 10              Total Cash In      0   4250   67947          67947
 11    ------------------------------------------------------------------
 12         CASH OUT - CAPITAL
 13    Factory machinery          0      0   15000
 14    Office machinery           0      0   30000
 15    (Spare)
 16              Total (A)        0      0   45000          45000
 17    ------------------------------------------------------------------
 18         CASH OUT - START UP
 19    Design of Widget Mk3       0      0
 20    (Spare)
 21              Total (B)        0      0                      0
 22    ------------------------------------------------------------------
 23      CASH OUT - VARIABLE DIRECT
 24    Parts for Widgets Mk1    800    854   12555
 25    Parts for Widgets Mk2    330    363    6115
 26    Diesel fuel (Deliveries)        0
 27    Wages (Temporary staff)    0      0
 28    (Spare)
 29              Total (C)     1130   1217   18670          18670
 30    ------------------------------------------------------------------
 31      CASH OUT - CONSTANT DIRECT
 32    Electricity                0      0
 33    Gas                        0      0
 34    Machine maintenance (Factory)     0      0
 35    Salaries (Widget production)      0      0
 36    Vehicle maintenance (Delivery)    0      0
 37    (Spare)
 38              Total (D)        0      0                      0
 39    ------------------------------------------------------------------
 40      CASH OUT - OVERHEADS
 41    Building maintenance       0      0
 42    Machine maintenance (Office)      0      0
 43    Petrol (Manager's cars)    0      0
 44    Postage                    0      0
 45    Rates                      0      0
 46    Salaries (Management)      0      0
 47    Stationery                 0      0
 48    Telephone                  0      0
 49    Vehicle maintenance (Managers)    0      0
 50    (Spare)
 51              Total (E)        0      0                      0
 52    ------------------------------------------------------------------
 53         TOTAL CASH OUT
 54         ( A+B+C+D+E )
 55              Total Cash Out (F)  1130   1217   63670      63670
 56    ==================================================================
 57      CASH FLOW AND BANK          Jan    Feb    Year
 58    ------------------------------------------------------------------
 59    Net cash flow           -1130   3033   4277           4277
 60    ------------------------------------------------------------------
 61    Balance B/F    Enter figure >>        -1130
 62    Cash In                    0   4250   67947
 63    Cash Out                1130   1217   63670
 64    Balance C/F             -1130   1903
 65    ==================================================================
```

The fundamental difference between a budget forecast and a cash flow forecast is *timing*, and, therefore, where appropriate, an offset between the budget and cash flow needs to be built in.

An offset is very easily provided. For instance, if we want March 'Sales' – which are in column D – to appear as 'Cash In' for April – which is column E – it is only necessary to link column E of the cash flow to column D of the budget.

> The fundamental difference between a budget forecast and a cash flow forecast is *timing*, and, therefore, where appropriate, an offset between the budget and cash flow needs to be built in.

Clearly the offsets used in the example can only be illustrative. In this area, more than any other, they are very much dependent upon the company's policy, the nature of their business, and the policy and behaviour of their customers and suppliers.

In the example then, offsets will be based on credible possibilities and explained as such, but unnecessary complexities will be avoided.

## Steps for creating the cash flow forecast

> All of the steps described below have been completed for ★**CASH01** on the illustration disc.

1 A cash flow forecast contains all of the cost and revenue headings that are in the budget, and so the easiest way to construct the framework for it is to copy the budget file, and then make the necessary modifications.
   Make a copy of file BUDG01 with the name CASH01

2 Change the file name in A1, and the top titles, as shown in Figure 6.4.

3 Delete the rows not required, remember that as soon as a row has been deleted the rest will automatically be re-numbered, as you can see in Figure 6.4, and so will no longer have the numbers shown below.
   The (original number) rows to delete are:

| | |
|---|---|
| 7 | Volume – Widgets Mk1 |
| 8 | Volume – Widgets Mk2 |
| 9 | (Spare) |
| 10 | Total volume |
| 11 | |
| 28 | VARIABLE DIRECT COSTS/ITEM |
| 29 | Parts for Widgets Mk1 |
| 30 | Parts for Widgets Mk2 |

| 31 | Diesel fuel (Deliveries) |
| 32 | Wages (Temporary staff) |
| 33 | (Spare) |
| 34 | |

| 36 | (Vol x Cost / Item) |

*Don't worry* that some rows now display an ERROR message, this is only because elements of their formulae have been deleted by removing the unwanted rows.

**4**  Change the row headings to match Figure 6.4.

### Linking to Sales and the Budget

### 5  CASH IN – SALES

We'll assume that the cash in from sales is received one month after the sale shown in the sales forecast, which means that we need a 'one month later' offset.

This model was copied from the budget forecast, and so there are already links to the sales forecast in rows 7 and 8, but they are not the ones we need, so delete all of the formulae from January to December in rows 7 and 8.

Because in this example there isn't a forecast for the previous year, no *cash in* for January can be shown, so the first link formulae will be in February – *column C*, as follows:

| *In cell* | *Heading* | *Enter* |
|---|---|---|
| C7 | From sales – Widgets Mk1 | SALES01!B16 |
| C8 | From sales – Widgets Mk2 | SALES01!B17 |

then copy them to the rest of the year.

### 6  CASH OUT – CAPITAL

For capital we will assume that cash is paid out in the same month as shown in the budget:

| *In cell* | *Heading* | *Enter* |
|---|---|---|
| B13 | Factory machinery | BUDG01!B18 |
| B14 | Office machinery | BUDG01!B19 |

then copy them to the rest of the year.

### 7  CASH OUT – START UP

For start up we will assume that cash is paid out in the same month as shown in the budget:

| In cell | Heading | Enter |
|---|---|---|
| B19 | Design of Widget Mk3 | BUDG01!B24 |

then copy it to the rest of the year.

## 8  CASH OUT – VARIABLE DIRECT

The offsets for variable direct costs are very much dependent upon their nature, and quite probably somewhat variable according to prevailing circumstances.

### Parts for widgets

We'll assume that parts are ordered and received one month before they are converted into finished widgets, and that it is another month before the widgets are sold. So parts are received *two months before* the widget appears in the sales forecast. The supplier invoices immediately on delivery to us, but allows 30 days for payment, thus the cash is paid out for them one month later, which is one month before they appear in the sales forecast. A table might help!

### Table 6.1  Paying for widget parts

|  | Jan | Feb | Mar |
|---|---|---|---|
| Part ordered and received ........................ | XX | | |
| Purchase invoice sent (30 days) .............. | XX | | |
| Parts used in manufacture ........................ | | XX | |
| Widget sales ............................................ | | | XX |
| Parts paid for ........................................... | | XX | |

Now, the cost of widget parts is calculated in the budget forecast, so we need to link the cash flow forecast to the budget forecast using an offset of *one month before*.

Delete the formulae that are already in January to December of rows 37 and 38. Then:

| In cell | Heading | Enter |
|---|---|---|
| B24 | Parts for Widgets Mk1 | BUDG01!C37 |
| B25 | Parts for Widgets Mk2 | BUDG01!C38 |

and copy them as far as *November*. We can't include December in the linking because that will refer to widget sales in January of the following year.

### Diesel fuel (Deliveries)

Diesel fuel for deliveries is bought in the same month as widgets are sold, and we'll assume that we receive 30 days' credit on its purchase. That means we pay for it one month after the sale, and thus the first payment in this forecast will not appear until February:

| In cell | Heading | Enter |
|---------|---------|-------|
| C26 | Diesel fuel (Deliveries) | BUDG01!B39 |

and copy to the end of the year.

### Wages (Temporary staff)

Wages are paid weekly, and the cost of them is incurred in line with sales, remember that these are temporary staff, taken on for packing and distribution of completed widgets. Strictly speaking then there should be a one week offset *after* sales. But the model is built on a monthly basis, so a one-week offset is not easily incorporated. If we assume that wages are paid in the same month as sales, we'll be right for three weeks of a four-week month, and that will be good enough for our purpose:

109

| In cell | Heading | Enter |
|---------|---------|-------|
| B27 | Wages (Temporary staff) | BUDG01!B40 |

and copy to the end of the year.

## 9 CASH OUT – CONSTANT DIRECT

For constant directs we'll assume that cash is paid out in the same month as they are shown in the budget:

| In cell | Heading | Enter |
|---------|---------|-------|
| B32 | Electricity | BUDG01!B45 |
| B33 | Gas | BUDG01!B46 |
| B34 | Machine maintenance (Factory) | BUDG01!B47 |
| B35 | Salaries (Widget production) | BUDG01!B48 |
| B36 | Vehicle maintenance (Delivery) | BUDG01!B49 |

and copy to the end of the year.

**Note:** Another quicker way to create all of these formulae is by entering only the first, in this case **BUDG01!B45** in B32, and copying it to the required rows and columns. But remember that you can only do it this way if all of the rows have the same offset. It wouldn't have worked for instance on the 'Variable Direct' block above, because the offsets for every row are not the same. It can be used for 'Overheads' below though.

### 10 CASH OUT – OVERHEADS

For overheads we'll assume that cash is paid out for all of them in the same month as they are shown in the budget. But bear in mind that any individual row, of any category, can be set for any other offset that may be appropriate:

| In cell | Heading | Enter |
|---------|---------|-------|
| B41 | Building maintenance | BUDG01!B54 |
| B42 | Machine maintenance (Office) | BUDG01!B55 |
| B43 | Petrol (Manager's cars) | BUDG01!B56 |
| B44 | Postage | BUDG01!B57 |
| B45 | Rates | BUDG01!B58 |
| B46 | Salaries (Management) | BUDG01!B59 |
| B47 | Stationery | BUDG01!B60 |
| B48 | Telephone | BUDG01!B61 |
| B49 | Vehicle maintenance (Managers) | BUDG01!B62 |

and copy to the end of the year.

### 11 CASH FLOW AND BANK

This block uses only spreadsheet links, that is, the references are to cells within the cash flow forecast.

#### Month headings

Because this spreadsheet is fairly long, it is helpful to have the month headings repeated somewhere near the bottom of the spreadsheet, so we'll put them in row 57, beside the heading 'Cash flow and bank'. It isn't necessary to type them all in again:

| In cell | Heading | Enter |
|---------|---------|-------|
| B57 | Cash flow and bank | B5 |

which is the cell address of 'Jan' at the top of the spreadsheet, and the text 'Jan' will be repeated. Then copy across the row to column N.

#### Net cash flow

Net cash flow is simply Cash In *minus* Cash Out:

| In cell | Heading | Enter |
|---------|---------|-------|
| B59 | Net cash flow | B10-B55 |

and copy for the rest of the year.

## Balance B/F

Balance brought forward is the previous month's balance carried forward. Because there is no forecast for the previous year, there is no balance brought forward in January and the first entry is therefore in February:

| In cell | Heading | Enter |
| --- | --- | --- |
| C61 | Balance B/F | B64 |

and copy for the rest of the year.

## Cash In and Cash Out

These are repeats of 'Total Cash In' and 'Total Cash Out' for the sake of clarity:

| In cell | Heading | Enter |
| --- | --- | --- |
| B62 | Cash In | B10 |
| B63 | Cash Out | B55 |

and copy for the rest of the year.

## Balance C/F

The balance is calculated by adding 'Cash In' to 'Balance B/F' and subtracting 'Cash Out':

| In cell | Heading | Enter |
| --- | --- | --- |
| B64 | Balance C/F | B61 + B62 + B63 |

and copy for the rest of the year.

## 12 CHECK SUM

The check sum that was copied in as part of the budget forecast needs to be modified to take account of the inclusion of Cash In:

Give the Cash In range B7:M9 the name **CHECKIN**.

| In cell | Enter |
| --- | --- |
| P10 | SUM(CHECKIN) |
| P59 | SUM(CHECKIN) – SUM(CHECKOUT) |
| A4 | IF(INT(N59)<>INT(P59),"!!!! CHECK SUM ERROR !!!!","") |

And that completes work on the cash flow forecast. Because it draws all of its data from either the *sales forecast* or the *budget forecast*, nothing more will need to be added, except for some dummy figures that will be put into the cells that are empty due to there being no forecasts for the previous or following years.

## Figure 6.5 (∗CASH01 – Formulae display)
## The formulae in the cash flow forecast

```
     I        A         II        B         II      C        II  O  II   P
 1   FILE : CASH01.xls            W I D G E T   M A K E R S   L T D
 2   = NOW ( )                    Cash Flow Forecast - 1997
 3   = TIME VALUE (A2)
 4   IF(INT(N59)<>INT(P59),'!!!! CHECK SUM ERROR !!!!','')
 5                                Jan               Feb                    Check
 6        CASH IN                                                          Sums
 7   From sales - Widgets Mk1                       SALES01!B16
 8   From sales - Widgets Mk2                       SALES01!B17
 9   (Spare)
10            Total Cash In   SUM(B7:B9)      SUM(C7:C9)      SUM(CHECKIN)
11   -----------------------------------------------------------------------------------
12        CASH OUT - CAPITAL
13   Factory machinery               BUDG01!B18      BUDG01!C18
14   Office machinery                BUDG01!B19      BUDG01!C19
15   (Spare)
16            Total (A)   SUM(B13:B15)    SUM(C13:C15)    SUM(CAPITAL)
17   -----------------------------------------------------------------------------------
18        CASH OUT - START UP
19   Design of Widget Mk3            BUDG01!B24      BUDG01!C24
20   (Spare)
21            Total (B)   SUM(B19:B20)    SUM(C19:C20)    SUM(STARTUP)
22   -----------------------------------------------------------------------------------
23        CASH OUT - VARIABLE DIRECT
24   Parts for Widgets Mk1           BUDG01!C37      SUDG01!D37
25   Parts for Widgets Mk2           BUDG01!C38      BUDG01!D38
26   Diesel fuel (Deliveries)        BUDG01!B39
27   Wages (Temporary staff)         BUDG01!B40      BUDG01!C40
28   (Spare)
29            Total (C)   SUM(B24:B28)    SUM(C24:C28)    SUM(VARIABLE)
30   -----------------------------------------------------------------------------------
31        CASH OUT - CONSTANT DIRECT
32   Electricity                     BUDG01!B45      BUDG01!C45
33   Gas                             BUDG01!B46      BUDG01!C46
34   Machine maintenance (Factory)   BUDG01!B47      BUDG01!C47
35   Salaries (Widget production)    BUDG01!B48      BUDG01!C48
36   Vehicle maintenance (Delivery)  BUDG01!B49      BUDG01!C49
37   (Spare)
38            Total (D)   SUM(B32:B37)    SUM(C32:C37)    SUM(CONSTANT)
39   -----------------------------------------------------------------------------------
40        CASH OUT - OVERHEADS
41   Building maintenance            BUDG01!B54      BUDG01!C54
42   Machine maintenance (Office)    BUDG01!B55      BUDG01!C55
43   Petrol (Manager's cars)         BUDG01!B56      BUDG01!C56
44   Postage                         BUDG01!B57      BUDG01!C57
45   Rates                           BUDG01!B58      BUDG01!C58
46   Salaries (Management)           BUDG01!B59      BUDG01!C59
47   Stationery                      BUDG01!B60      BUDG01!C60
48   Telephone                       BUDG01!B61      BUDG01!C61
49   Vehicle maintenance (Managers)  BUDG01!B62      BUDG01!C62
50   (Spare)
51            Total (E)   SUM(B41:B50)    SUM(C41:C50)    SUM(OVERHEADS)
52   -----------------------------------------------------------------------------------
53        TOTAL CASH OUT
54        ( A+B+C+D+E )
55            Total Cash Out (F)  B16+B21+B29+B38+B51  C16+C21+C29+C38+C51SUM(CHECKOUT)
56   =================================================================================
57        CASH FLOW AND BANK              B5              C5
58   -----------------------------------------------------------------------------------
59   Net cash flow                   B10-B55         C10-C55         SUM(CHECKIN)-SUM(CHECKOUT)
60   -----------------------------------------------------------------------------------
61   Balance B/F    Enter figure >>                  B64
62   Cash In                         B10             C10
63   Cash Out                        B55             C55
64   Balance C/F                     B61+B62-B63     C61+C62-C63
65   =================================================================================
```

**Figure 6.6 Cash flow offsets**

```
                                    Jan         Feb
                   CASH IN
    7    From sales - Widgets Mk          ◄────────O
    8    From sales - Widgets Mk2         ◄────────O

   11    ------------------------------------------------
   12          CASH OUT - CAPITAL
   13    Factory machinery                    ↑          ↑
   14    Office machinery                     ↑          ↑

   17    ------------------------------------------------
   18          CASH OUT - START UP
   19    Design of Widget Mk3                 ↑          ↑

   22    ------------------------------------------------
   23     CASH OUT - VARIABLE DIRECT
   24    Parts for Widgets Mk1            O────────►
   25    Parts for Widgets Mk2            O────────►
   26    Diesel fuel (Deliveries)         ◄────────O
   27    Wages (Temporary staff)              ↑          ↑

   30    ------------------------------------------------
   31     CASH OUT - CONSTANT DIRECT
   32    Electricity                          ↑          ↑
   33    Gas                                  ↑          ↑
   34    Machine maintenance (Factory)        ↑          ↑
   35    Salaries (Widget production)         ↑          ↑
   36    Vehicle maintenance (Delivery)       ↑          ↑

   39    ------------------------------------------------
   40          CASH OUT - OVERHEADS
   41    Building maintenance                 ↑          ↑
   42    Machine maintenance (Office)         ↑          ↑
   43    Petrol (Manager's cars)              ↑          ↑
   44    Postage                              ↑          ↑
   45    Rates                                ↑          ↑
   46    Salaries (Management)                ↑          ↑
   47    Stationery                           ↑          ↑
   48    Telephone                            ↑          ↑
   49    Vehicle maintenance (Managers)       ↑          ↑
```

113

Finally, a summary table of the offsets used in the cash flow might be a useful *aide-mémoire* (see Figure 6.6, page 113). The arrows point to the source column (month) in either the sales or budget forecasts, an up arrow ↑ indicates that the link is to the same month.

## Summary

In this chapter:

- a sales forecast framework with the file name SALES01 was created;
- a budget forecast framework with the file name BUDG01 was created, with links back to the sales forecast to enable automatic update of revenue and variable direct costs when the sales forecast is altered;
- a cash flow forecast framework with the file name CASH01 was created. It has links to both the sales and budget forecasts, and requires no additional data entry, except for dummy figures for the bank 'Balance B/F' and other cells that normally rely on the existence of forecasts for the previous and following years.

# PART 4

. . .

# Using the forecast

The budget forecast frameworks are now ready for use. Part 4 will deal with the financial aspects of making the forecasts, and the reiterative process of fine tuning them. Subsequential departmental budget allocations are considered.

The ways in which forecasts can be reviewed using actual performance data will be discussed, together with the implications of review on the remainder of the forecast year.

Key ratios, which are shorthand means of monitoring performance, will be introduced and incorporated in the forecast.

Profitability of both the whole company, and of individual products, will be examined.

The use of graphs (charts) will be introduced as necessary where their form of information presentation becomes beneficial.

**Note:** All monetary figures exclude Value Added Tax unless explicitly stated otherwise.

---

**Note for users of the illustration disc.** Now that the basic frameworks are built, you can choose to either enter figures or any additional features into them yourself on the files named in the book. Or, if you prefer, refer to the preprepared spreadsheets provided on the illustration disc. The preprepared versions are identified by a suffix P in the file name. They are now complete, including additional facilities that will be described later in the book.

Monitoring, comparing, reviewing and reforecasting are the essential and most prominent features of budget forecasts. It is worth repeating the truism that 'There is only one certainty in a forecast – it is wrong', and the task of all concerned with it is to continually compare it with actual performance and refine it for the best possible accuracy.

# 7
. . .

# Assembling the budget

Making the sales forecast ■   117

Making the budget forecast ■

Cash flow forecast adjustments ■

Graphs and key indicators ■

Key ratios ■

# Making the sales forecast

■ ■ ■

In the case of Widget Makers Ltd there are only two products to consider – Widgets Mk1 and Widgets Mk2. All that is needed are entries for each product in each month of the sales forecast's span: one year.

Entering the figures only takes a few seconds, of course. By far the greatest proportion of the task of forecasting sales draws on the experience and expertise of the company's managers and sales force, and the many factors that will be considered in their deliberations.

The principal contribution that spreadsheet forecasts and budgets make to the science (or art?) of marketing and selling is the facility of instantly testing the financial impact of any sales profile that may be imagined. And this can have the most profound effect on the way in which forecasting is carried out and sales targets are set. For instance, the individual and overall impact on profitability of various product sales volumes can be quickly tested, and this may result in a radically different sales policy and strategy as compared with that based on minimal testing, or indeed wholly gut feeling.

All of this suggests that the budget forecasting process is one of reiteration, rather than a single run through from start to finish, and in fact, that is the case throughout. When we look at monitoring and reviewing later on we will see that these are also a process of reiteration.

Monitoring, comparing, reviewing and reforecasting are the essential and most prominent features of budget forecasts. It is worth repeating the truism that 'There is only one certainty in a forecast – it is wrong', and the task of all concerned with it is to continually compare it with actual performance and refine it for the best possible accuracy.

Thus, the figures that we are about to enter may be considered a first stab, which will almost certainly be modified several times once the rest of the budget is finished and their effect seen.

We will assume that at least all of the following have been taken into account in deciding the first shot at the sales volumes for the year:

■ economic factors;

■ factors affecting the industry sector;

■ seasonal factors;

■ the company's growth policy;

■ capital investment plans;

■ marketing strategy plans;

■ production capability;

- financing arrangements;
- market sector competition.

And having considered them, we decide to first of all see how a flat profile will look, based on the average sales for each product for the previous year:

Average sales/month – Widgets Mk1 : 200
Average sales/month – Widgets Mk2 : 100

The pricing policy must also be decided; whether to increase, decrease, or maintain the previous year's prices. Many of the sales volume factors above will also have a bearing on the pricing decision, and, certainly as much as for sales volumes, the process of reiteration will be used before finalising it.

We will assume that Widgets Mk1 are the longer established of the two products, have less facility than Widgets Mk2, and are cheaper to produce. The selling price for the first run through the budget will be:

Sales price of Widgets Mk1 : £275.00
Sales price of Widgets Mk2 : £400.00

119

These figures can now be entered on the spreadsheet.

Before they are, make a *save* copy of the sales forecast, with a new file extension. I have used SALES01.SV1 on the illustration disc. In this way, if any of the changes introduced turn out to be not wanted after all, making another copy of the .SV file with the original file extension (xls for Excel, .wk1 or .wks for Lotus 1-2-3 for example) will restore the status quo. An easy and foolproof way of making a 'save' copy:

**a** Load the file of which a save copy is required.
**b** Select FILE, SAVE AS and change the file extension to **.SV1**, and 'save' it.
**c** Close the spreadsheet.

---

★**SALES01** to enter the figures yourself, or ★**SALES01P** for the preprepared version.

### Figure 7.1 (∗SALES01) The completed sales forecast

| | A | B | C | D | E | F | G | |
|---|---|---|---|---|---|---|---|---|
| 1 | FILE : SALES01.xls | | W I D G E T | M A K E R S | L T D | | | |
| 2 | 06/09/96 | | | Sales Forecast 1997 | | | | |
| 3 | 14:59 | | | | | | | |
| 4 | ∗∗∗ SALES ∗∗∗ | Jan | Feb | Mar | Apr | May | Jun | |
| 5 | Volume | | | | | | | |
| 6 | Widgets Mk1 | 200 | 200 | 200 | 200 | 200 | 200 | |
| 7 | Widgets Mk2 | 100 | 100 | 100 | 100 | 100 | 100 | |
| 8 | (Spare) | | | | | | | |
| 9 | Total Volume | 300 | 300 | 300 | 300 | 300 | 300 | |
| 10 | | | | | | | | |
| 11 | Price (£) | | | | | | | |
| 12 | Widgets Mk1 | 275 | 275 | 275 | 275 | 275 | 275 | |
| 13 | Widgets Mk2 | 400 | 400 | 400 | 400 | 400 | 400 | |
| 14 | | | | | | | | |
| 15 | Sales Value (£) | | | | | | | |
| 16 | Widgets Mk1 | 55000 | 55000 | 55000 | 55000 | 55000 | 55000 | 5 |
| 17 | Widgets Mk2 | 40000 | 40000 | 40000 | 40000 | 40000 | 40000 | 4 |
| 18 | (Spare) | | | | | | | |
| 19 | Total Value | 95000 | 95000 | 95000 | 95000 | 95000 | 95000 | 9 |

Right, that's the sales forecast done, now we'll move on to the budget.

## Making the budget forecast

■ ■ ■

Bearing in mind that the process of making a budget is one of reiteration, should all of the costs be put in at this stage, or only those that affect trading profitability, and then add non-trading expenditure like capital and start up later? It really doesn't matter at all, because it's so easy to change things around; add and remove costs, alter prices and volumes, and so on, as much as you want.

For Widget Makers Ltd we'll put everything in to start with, and see how the budget and cash flow look before considering changes.

Figure 7.2 (see page 122) shows the budget spreadsheet after entry of all of the figures.

It doesn't matter in what order cost decisions and entries into the spreadsheet are made, but we'll take them as they appear on the budget forecast model, in cost category order.

The detail of the entries given for each heading below are repeated in a summary for the whole budget at the end of the section.

---

★**BUDG01** to enter the figures yourself, or ★**BUDG01P** for the preprepared version.

---

# Capital costs

These are items of expenditure that have a realisable value, they are assets of the company.

## Factory machinery

A new widget manufacturing machine will be bought in March at a cost of £50,000. The new machine will enable widget production volumes to increase without the need for additional production staff once it has been brought into service in September. Until then, monthly production volumes cannot increase more than 10 per cent above those in January at the start of the year. Enter:

| Row | Heading | Month(s) | £ |
|-----|---------|----------|---|
| 18 | Factory machinery | Mar | 50000 |

## Office machinery

A replacement photocopier is needed, and will be bought in May at a cost of £5,000. In October a new computer system will be installed that will enable administration costs to be contained in following years as the business grows. Enter:

| Row | Heading | Month(s) | £ |
|-----|---------|----------|---|
| 19 | Office machinery | May | 5000 |
| | | Oct | 25000 |

# Start up costs

These are 'one off' items of expenditure incurred solely through the development or introduction of a new product.

121

## Figure 7.2 (∗BUDG01)
## The completed budget forecast

|  | A | Jan | Feb | Mar | Apr | May | Jun |
|---|---|---|---|---|---|---|---|
| 1 | FILE : BUDG01.xls | | | WIDGET MAKERS LTD | | | |
| 2 | 21/10/1996 | | | Budget Forecast - 1997 | | | |
| 3 | 8:56am | | | | | | |
| 4 | | | | | | | |
| 5 | | Jan | Feb | Mar | Apr | May | Jun |
| 6 | SALES | | | | | | |
| 7 | Volume - Widgets Mk1 | 200 | 200 | 200 | 200 | 200 | 200 |
| 8 | Volume - Widgets Mk2 | 100 | 100 | 100 | 100 | 100 | 100 |
| 9 | (Spare) | | | | | | |
| 10 | Total volume | 300 | 300 | 300 | 300 | 300 | 300 |
| 11 | | | | | | | |
| 12 | Value - Widgets Mk1 | 55000 | 55000 | 55000 | 55000 | 55000 | 55000 |
| 13 | Value - Widgets Mk2 | 40000 | 40000 | 40000 | 40000 | 40000 | 40000 |
| 14 | (Spare) | | | | | | |
| 15 | Total £ Value | 95000 | 95000 | 95000 | 95000 | 95000 | 95000 |
| 16 | | | | | | | |
| 17 | CAPITAL COSTS | | | | | | |
| 18 | Factory machinery | | | 50000 | | | |
| 19 | Office machinery | | | | | 5000 | |
| 20 | (Spare) | | | | | | |
| 21 | Total (A) | 0 | 0 | 50000 | 0 | 5000 | 0 |
| 22 | | | | | | | |
| 23 | START UP COSTS | | | | | | |
| 24 | Design of Widget Mk3 | | | | 10000 | 2000 | 2000 |
| 25 | (Spare) | | | | | | |
| 26 | Total (B) | 0 | 0 | 0 | 10000 | 2000 | 2000 |
| 27 | | | | | | | |
| 28 | VARIABLE DIRECT COSTS / ITEM | | | | | | |
| 29 | Parts for Widgets Mk1 | 140 | 140 | 140 | 140 | 140 | 140 |
| 30 | Parts for Widgets Mk2 | 160 | 160 | 160 | 160 | 160 | 160 |
| 31 | Diesel fuel (Deliveries) | 8 | 8 | 8 | 8 | 8 | 8 |
| 32 | Wages (Temporary staff) | 15 | 15 | 15 | 15 | 15 | 15 |
| 33 | (Spare) | | | | | | |
| 34 | | | | | | | |
| 35 | VARIABLE DIRECT COSTS | | | | | | |
| 36 | (Vol x Cost / Item) | | | | | | |
| 37 | Parts for Widgets Mk1 | 28000 | 28000 | 28000 | 28000 | 28000 | 28000 |
| 38 | Parts for Widgets Mk2 | 16000 | 16000 | 16000 | 16000 | 16000 | 16000 |
| 39 | Diesel fuel (Deliveries) | 2400 | 2400 | 2400 | 2400 | 2400 | 2400 |
| 40 | Wages (Temporary staff) | 4500 | 4500 | 4500 | 4500 | 4500 | 4500 |
| 41 | (Spare) | | | | | | |
| 42 | Total (C) | 50900 | 50900 | 50900 | 50900 | 50900 | 50900 |
| 43 | | | | | | | |
| 44 | CONSTANT DIRECT COSTS | | | | | | |
| 45 | Electricity | | 500 | | | 500 | |
| 46 | Gas | | | 900 | | | 700 |
| 47 | Machine maintenance (Factory) | 600 | 600 | 600 | 600 | 600 | 600 |
| 48 | Salaries (Widget production) | 20000 | 20000 | 20000 | 20000 | 20000 | 20000 |
| 49 | Vehicle maintenance (Delivery) | 300 | 300 | 300 | 300 | 300 | 300 |
| 50 | (Spare) | | | | | | |
| 51 | Total (D) | 20900 | 21400 | 21800 | 20900 | 21400 | 21600 |
| 52 | | | | | | | |
| 53 | OVERHEADS | | | | | | |
| 54 | Building maintenance | 400 | 400 | 400 | 400 | 2900 | 400 |
| 55 | Machine maintenance (Office) | 100 | 100 | 100 | 100 | 100 | 100 |
| 56 | Petrol (Manager's cars) | 600 | 600 | 600 | 600 | 600 | 600 |
| 57 | Postage | 90 | 90 | 90 | 90 | 90 | 90 |
| 58 | Rates | 200 | | | 200 | 200 | 200 |
| 59 | Salaries (Management) | 17000 | 1 000 | 17000 | 17000 | 17000 | 17000 |
| 60 | Stationery | 85 | 85 | 85 | 85 | 85 | 85 |
| 61 | Telephone | | 325 | | | 325 | |
| 62 | Vehicle maintenance (Managers) | 100 | 100 | 100 | 100 | 100 | 100 |
| 63 | (Spare) | | | | | | |
| 64 | Total (E) | 18575 | 18700 | 18375 | 18575 | 21400 | 18575 |
| 65 | | | | | | | |
| 66 | TOTAL COSTS | | | | | | |
| 67 | ( A+B+C+D+E ) | | | | | | |
| 68 | Total (F) | 90375 | 91000 | 141075 | 100375 | 100700 | 93075 |
| 69 | | | | | | | |

| H | | I | | J | | K | | L | | M | | N | | O | | P | |
|---|---|---|---|---|---|---|---|---|---|---|---|---|---|---|---|---|---|

| Jul | Aug | Sep | Oct | Nov | Dec | Year | | Check Sums |
|---|---|---|---|---|---|---|---|---|
| 200 | 200 | 200 | 200 | 200 | 200 | 2400 | | |
| 100 | 100 | 100 | 100 | 100 | 100 | 1200 | | |
| 300 | 300 | 300 | 300 | 300 | 300 | 3600 | | |
| 55000 | 55000 | 55000 | 55000 | 55000 | 55000 | 660000 | | |
| 40000 | 40000 | 40000 | 40000 | 40000 | 40000 | 480000 | | |
| 95000 | 95000 | 95000 | 95000 | 95000 | 95000 | 1140000 | | |
| | | | | | | 50000 | | |
| | | | 25000 | | | 30000 | | |
| 0 | 0 | 0 | 25000 | 0 | 0 | 80000 | | 80000 |
| 2000 | 2000 | 2000 | 2000 | 2000 | 2000 | 26000 | | |
| 2000 | 2000 | 2000 | 2000 | 2000 | 2000 | 26000 | | 26000 |
| 140 | 140 | 140 | 140 | 140 | 140 | | | |
| 160 | 160 | 160 | 160 | 160 | 160 | | | |
| 8 | 8 | 8 | 8 | 8 | 8 | | | |
| 15 | 15 | 15 | 15 | 15 | 15 | | | |
| 28000 | 28000 | 28000 | 28000 | 28000 | 28000 | 336000 | | |
| 16000 | 16000 | 16000 | 16000 | 16000 | 16000 | 192000 | | |
| 2400 | 2400 | 2400 | 2400 | 2400 | 2400 | 28800 | | |
| 4500 | 4500 | 4500 | 4500 | 4500 | 4500 | 54000 | | |
| 50900 | 50900 | 50900 | 50900 | 50900 | 50900 | 610800 | | 610800 |
| | 500 | | | 500 | | 2000 | | |
| | | 200 | | | 700 | 2500 | | |
| 600 | 600 | 600 | 600 | 600 | 600 | 7200 | | |
| 20000 | 20000 | 20000 | 20000 | 20000 | 20000 | 240000 | | |
| 300 | 300 | 300 | 300 | 300 | 300 | 3600 | | |
| 20900 | 21400 | 21100 | 20900 | 21400 | 21600 | 255300 | | 255300 |
| 400 | 400 | 400 | 400 | 400 | 400 | 7300 | | |
| 100 | 100 | 100 | 100 | 100 | 100 | 1200 | | |
| 600 | 600 | 600 | 600 | 600 | 600 | 7200 | | |
| 90 | 90 | 90 | 90 | 90 | 90 | 1080 | | |
| 200 | 200 | 200 | 200 | 200 | 200 | 2000 | | |
| 17000 | 17000 | 17000 | 17000 | 17000 | 17000 | 204000 | | |
| 85 | 85 | 85 | 85 | 85 | 85 | 1020 | | |
| | 325 | | | 325 | | 1300 | | |
| 100 | 100 | 100 | 100 | 100 | 100 | 1200 | | |
| 18575 | 18900 | 18575 | 18575 | 18900 | 18575 | 226300 | | 226300 |
| 92375 | 93200 | 92575 | 117375 | 93200 | 93075 | 1198400 | | 1198400 |

123

### Design of Widget Mk3

In this case a new widget, the Mk3, is being developed. There is an initial cost of £10,000 for engineering design consultancy in April, then a monthly design development cost of £2,000 for the remainder of the year. Enter:

| Row | Heading | Month(s) | £ |
|---|---|---|---|
| 24 | Design of Widget Mk3 | Apr | 10000 |
| | | May – Dec | 2000 |

## Variable direct costs/item

These are the costs per widget, which are multiplied by the widget volumes to generate the variable direct costs. The formulae that carry out this calculation were put into the spreadsheet in Chapter 6.

### Parts for widgets

For now, assume a constant cost of parts throughout the year, although it is possible that a change may have to be made later on. The cost of parts for Widgets Mk2 are higher than those of the Mk1. Enter:

| Row | Heading | Month(s) | £ |
|---|---|---|---|
| 29 | Parts for Widgets Mk1 | Jan – Dec | 140 |
| 30 | Parts for Widgets Mk2 | Jan – Dec | 160 |

### Diesel fuel (Deliveries)

This is the fuel used by the vehicles delivering widgets to customers. In a new business the cost per widget would at this stage be an estimate, but in an established business the figure is easily derived by dividing the previous year's total cost of diesel fuel by the number of widgets delivered during that year. Enter:

| Row | Heading | Month(s) | £ |
|---|---|---|---|
| 31 | Diesel fuel (Deliveries) | Jan – Dec | 8 |

### Wages (Temporary staff)

These wages are for temporary staff taken on as, and when, required to assist with widget packing and delivery. Again, for a new business the figure per widget will be an estimate, or in an established business, calculated by dividing the previous year's total cost of temporary staff's wages by the widget volumes for that year. Enter:

| Row | Heading | Month(s) | £ |
|---|---|---|---|
| 32 | Wages (Temporary staff) | Jan – Dec | 15 |

# Constant direct costs

These are the costs directly associated with the products, but not immediately affected by normal fluctuations in volume.

## Electricity

Used for lighting and machinery operation. Although the amount used is somewhat dependent upon production volumes, the swing is not that significant, and a value based upon the annual production volumes is good enough for the purpose of the budget. Enter:

| Row | Heading | Month(s) | £ |
|---|---|---|---|
| 45 | Electricity | Feb | 500 |
| | | May | 500 |
| | | Aug | 500 |
| | | Nov | 500 |

## Gas

Used predominantly for factory heating, the quarterly bills reflect seasonal requirements. Enter:

| Row | Heading | Month(s) | £ |
|---|---|---|---|
| 46 | Gas | Mar | 900 |
| | | Jun | 700 |
| | | Sep | 200 |
| | | Dec | 700 |

## Machine maintenance (Factory)

The factory machines are routinely maintained under contract covering both parts and labour. The contract terms require a monthly payment. Enter:

| Row | Heading | Month(s) | £ |
|---|---|---|---|
| 47 | Machine mt'ce (Factory) | Jan – Dec | 600 |

## Salaries (Widget production)

These are the salaries of all full-time staff directly involved in widget production. Enter:

| Row | Heading | Month(s) | £ |
|---|---|---|---|
| 48 | Salaries (Widget production) | Jan – Dec | 20000 |

### Vehicle maintenance (Delivery)

Although regular mileage services can be forecast to specific months, there are also irregular breakdowns to allow for. One way of handling any expense where the value can be anticipated, but the 'when' is unknown, is to derive an annual figure and spread it evenly through the year. Then, each month when actual expenditure is monitored, either forward any 'unused' portion of the figure to the next month, or once again spread it over what remains of the year. Using this method, enter:

| Row | Heading | Month(s) | £ |
|---|---|---|---|
| 49 | Vehicle mt'ce (Delivery) | Jan – Dec | 300 |

## Overhead costs

These are all trading costs not directly related to a product, and which are also neither capital nor start up.

### Building maintenance

This consists principally of factory and office cleaning which is invoiced monthly, but in addition, external painting will be carried out in the early summer. Enter:

| Row | Heading | Month(s) | £ |
|---|---|---|---|
| 54 | Building maintenance | Jan – Apr | 400 |
| | | Jun – Dec | 400 |
| | | May | 2900 |

> *Tip:* Put the May figures in as **400 + 2500**, this will act as a reminder that there are two components to the cost.

### Machine maintenance (Office)

Photocopiers, computers, fax and telex machines are all maintained under a maintenance contract that covers parts and labour for a monthly premium. Enter:

| Row | Heading | Month(s) | £ |
|---|---|---|---|
| 55 | Machine maintenance (Office) | Jan – Dec | 100 |

### Petrol (Managers' cars)

Although there will obviously be fluctuations in this expense from month to month, they are very difficult to predict, and in any case are small compared with the total overheads. An annual spread of the year's total forecast expenditure on petrol is, therefore, quite satisfactory. Enter:

| Row | Heading | Month(s) | £ |
|-----|---------|----------|---|
| 56 | Petrol (Managers' cars) | Jan – Dec | 600 |

## Postage

Like most other general administration costs, fluctuations in monthly costs are comparatively inconsequential and the year's forecast total may be spread throughout the year. Enter:

| Row | Heading | Month(s) | £ |
|-----|---------|----------|---|
| 57 | Postage | Jan – Dec | 90 |

## Rates

Business rates are usually paid monthly for ten months of the year, from April to January, inclusive. Enter:

| Row | Heading | Month(s) | £ |
|-----|---------|----------|---|
| 58 | Rates | Jan | 200 |
|  |  | Apr – Dec | 200 |

## Salaries (Management)

These are the salaries of managers and staff not directly involved in production. They include all additional costs such as National Insurance and pension contributions, although it may normally be preferable to separately identify those components, as it would also be for other extras such as bonus and productivity payments. Enter:

| Row | Heading | Month(s) | £ |
|-----|---------|----------|---|
| 59 | Salaries (Management) | Jan – Dec | 17000 |

## Stationery

For the same reasons as for postage, an even spread of the forecast annual cost will be satisfactory. Enter:

| Row | Heading | Month(s) | £ |
|-----|---------|----------|---|
| 60 | Stationery | Jan – Dec | 85 |

## Telephone

The telephone bill is paid quarterly, and although there are minor seasonal fluctuations, the year's forecast split equally into four payments is suitable for our needs. Enter:

| Row | Heading | Month(s) | £ |
|-----|---------|----------|---|
| 61 | Telephone | Feb | 325 |
|  |  | May | 325 |
|  |  | Aug | 325 |
|  |  | Nov | 325 |

### Vehicle maintenance (Managers)

In exactly the same way as for the delivery vehicle maintenance, an esti-mate of the total annual cost spread throughout the year will be satisfac-tory, so long as any unspent 'allocation' is rolled on from month to month. Enter:

| Row | Heading | Month(s) | £ |
|---|---|---|---|
| 62 | Vehicle mt'ce (Managers) | Jan – Dec | 100 |

And that completes the data entry for the budget forecast. A summary table of all of them can be found opposite.

# Cash flow forecast adjustments
■  ■  ■

The cash flow forecast is fully automatic in the sense that all of its data is drawn from either the sales or budget forecast. But, because in the example there are no forecasts for the previous or following year, and because of the offsets that have been built into it, there are some gaps in the cash flow for January and December.

This can of course also happen in real forecasts, when, for instance, the first computer-based forecast is constructed there will be none for the pre-vious year, nor indeed any for the following year. Therefore, a way is needed of dealing with that situation, in a way that maintains the forecast close to reality, without the need for continual checking and intervention.

The solution is to pick up the figures in the adjacent month, so that when they are changed during the reiterative process of forecasting, the dummy figures will also change. Some modification to this principle may be necessary if significant differences in adjacent months are expected for the heading in question. In the case of Widget Makers Ltd, the adjacent month method will work well enough for illustrative purposes.

The gaps, as the cash flow forecast currently stands, are:

| Row | Heading | Jan | Dec |
|---|---|---|---|
| 7 | From sales – Widgets Mk1 | XX | |
| 8 | From sales – Widgets Mk2 | XX | |
| 24 | Parts for Widgets Mk1 | | XX |
| 25 | Parts for Widgets Mk2 | | XX |
| 26 | Diesel fuel (Deliveries) | XX | |
| 61 | Balance B/F | XX | |

**Table 7.1  Summary of all budget data entries**

| Row | Heading | Month(s) | £ |
|-----|---------|----------|---|
| 18 | Factory machinery | Mar | 50000 |
| 19 | Office machinery | May | 5000 |
| 10 | Office machinery | Oct | 25000 |
| 24 | Design of Widget Mk3 | Apr | 10000 |
| 24 | Design of Widget Mk3 | May – Dec | 2000 |
| 29 | Parts for Widgets Mk1 | Jan – Dec | 140 |
| 30 | Parts for Widgets Mk2 | Jan – Dec | 160 |
| 31 | Diesel fuel (Deliveries) | Jan – Dec | 8 |
| 32 | Wages (Temporary staff) | Jan – Dec | 15 |
| 45 | Electricity | Feb | 500 |
| 45 | Electricity | May | 500 |
| 45 | Electricity | Aug | 500 |
| 45 | Electricity | Nov | 500 |
| 46 | Gas | Mar | 900 |
| 46 | Gas | Jun | 700 |
| 46 | Gas | Sep | 200 |
| 46 | Gas | Dec | 700 |
| 47 | Machine mt'ce (Factory) | Jan – Dec | 600 |
| 48 | Salaries (Widget production) | Jan – Dec | 20000 |
| 49 | Vehicle mt'ce (Delivery) | Jan – Dec | 300 |
| 54 | Building maintenance | Jan – Apr | 400 |
| 54 | Building maintenance | Jun – Dec | 400 |
| 54 | Building maintenance | May | 2900 |
| 55 | Machine maintenance (Office) | Jan – Dec | 100 |
| 56 | Petrol (Managers' cars) | Jan – Dec | 600 |
| 57 | Postage | Jan – Dec | 90 |
| 58 | Rates | Jan | 200 |
| 58 | Rates | Apr – Dec | 200 |
| 59 | Salaries (Management) | Jan – Dec | 17000 |
| 60 | Stationery | Jan – Dec | 85 |
| 61 | Telephone | Feb | 325 |
| 61 | Telephone | May | 325 |
| 61 | Telephone | Aug | 325 |
| 61 | Telephone | Nov | 325 |
| 62 | Vehicle mt'ce (Managers) | Jan – Dec | 100 |

## Figure 7.3 (∗CASH01)  The completed cash flow forecast

| | A | | B | C | D | E | F | G |
|---|---|---|---|---|---|---|---|---|
| 1 | FILE : CASH01.xls | | | | | | | |
| 2 | 21/10/1996 | | | WIDGET MAKERS LTD | | | | |
| 3 | 8:57am | | | Cash Flow Forecast - 1997 | | | | |
| 4 | | | | | | | | |
| 5 | | | Jan | Feb | Mar | Apr | May | Jun |
| 6 | CASH IN | | | | | | | |
| 7 | From sales - Widgets Mk1 | | 55000 | 55000 | 55000 | 55000 | 55000 | 55000 |
| 8 | From sales - Widgets Mk2 | | 40000 | 40000 | 40000 | 40000 | 40000 | 40000 |
| 9 | (Spare) | | | | | | | |
| 10 | Total Cash In | | 95000 | 95000 | 95000 | 95000 | 95000 | 95000 |
| 11 | --- | | | | | | | |
| 12 | CASH OUT - CAPITAL | | | | | | | |
| 13 | Factory machinery | | 0 | 0 | 50000 | 0 | 0 | 0 |
| 14 | Office machinery | | 0 | 0 | 0 | 0 | 5000 | 0 |
| 15 | (Spare) | | | | | | | |
| 16 | Total (A) | | 0 | 0 | 50000 | 0 | 5000 | 0 |
| 17 | --- | | | | | | | |
| 18 | CASH OUT - START UP | | | | | | | |
| 19 | Design of Widget Mk3 | | 0 | 0 | 0 | 10000 | 2000 | 2000 |
| 20 | (Spare) | | | | | | | |
| 21 | Total (B) | | 0 | 0 | 0 | 10000 | 2000 | 2000 |
| 22 | --- | | | | | | | |
| 23 | CASH OUT - VARIABLE DIRECT | | | | | | | |
| 24 | Parts for Widgets Mk1 | | 28000 | 28000 | 28000 | 28000 | 28000 | 28000 |
| 25 | Parts for Widgets Mk2 | | 16000 | 16000 | 16000 | 16000 | 16000 | 16000 |
| 26 | Diesel fuel (Deliveries) | | 2400 | 2400 | 2400 | 2400 | 2400 | 2400 |
| 27 | Wages (Temporary staff) | | 4500 | 4500 | 4500 | 4500 | 4500 | 4500 |
| 28 | (Spare) | | | | | | | |
| 29 | Total (C) | | 50900 | 50900 | 50900 | 50900 | 50900 | 50900 |
| 30 | --- | | | | | | | |
| 31 | CASH OUT - CONSTANT DIRECT | | | | | | | |
| 32 | Electricity | | 0 | 500 | 0 | 0 | 500 | 0 |
| 33 | Gas | | 0 | 0 | 900 | 0 | 0 | 700 |
| 34 | Machine maintenance (Factory) | | 600 | 600 | 600 | 600 | 600 | 600 |
| 35 | Salaries (Widget production) | | 20000 | 20000 | 20000 | 20000 | 20000 | 20000 |
| 36 | Vehicle maintenance (Delivery) | | 300 | 300 | 300 | 300 | 300 | 300 |
| 37 | (Spare) | | | | | | | |
| 38 | Total (D) | | 20900 | 21400 | 21800 | 20900 | 21400 | 21600 |
| 39 | --- | | | | | | | |
| 40 | CASH OUT - OVERHEADS | | | | | | | |
| 41 | Building maintenance | | 400 | 400 | 400 | 400 | 2900 | 400 |
| 42 | Machine maintenance (Office) | | 100 | 100 | 100 | 100 | 100 | 100 |
| 43 | Petrol (Manager's cars) | | 600 | 600 | 600 | 600 | 600 | 600 |
| 44 | Postage | | 90 | 90 | 90 | 90 | 90 | 90 |
| 45 | Rates | | 200 | 0 | 0 | 200 | 200 | 200 |
| 46 | Salaries (Management) | | 17000 | 17000 | 17000 | 17000 | 17000 | 17000 |
| 47 | Stationery | | 85 | 85 | 85 | 85 | 85 | 85 |
| 48 | Telephone | | 0 | 325 | 0 | 0 | 325 | 0 |
| 49 | Vehicle maintenance (Managers) | | 100 | 100 | 100 | 100 | 100 | 100 |
| 50 | (Spare) | | | | | | | |
| 51 | Total (E) | | 18575 | 18700 | 18375 | 18575 | 21400 | 18575 |
| 52 | --- | | | | | | | |
| 53 | TOTAL CASH OUT | | | | | | | |
| 54 | ( A+B+C+D+E ) | | | | | | | |
| 55 | Total Cash Out (F) | | 90375 | 91000 | 141075 | 100375 | 100700 | 93075 |
| 56 | === | | | | | | | |
| 57 | CASH FLOW AND BANK | | Jan | Feb | Mar | Apr | May | Jun |
| 58 | --- | | | | | | | |
| 59 | Net cash flow | | 4625 | 4000 | -46075 | -9375 | -5700 | 1925 |
| 60 | --- | | | | | | | |
| 61 | Balance B/F   Enter figure >> | | 35000 | 39625 | 43625 | -2450 | -7825 | -13525 |
| 62 | Cash In | | 95000 | 95000 | 95000 | 95000 | 95000 | 95000 |
| 63 | Cash Out | | 90375 | 91000 | 141075 | 100375 | 100700 | 93075 |
| 64 | Balance C/F | | 39625 | 43625 | -2450 | -7825 | -13525 | -11600 |
| 65 | === | | | | | | | |

| H || | I || | J || | K || | L || | M || | N || | O || | P | |
|---|---|---|---|---|---|---|---|
| Jul | Aug | Sep | Oct | Nov | Dec | Year | Check Sums |
| 55000 | 55000 | 55000 | 55000 | 55000 | 55000 | 660000 | |
| 40000 | 40000 | 40000 | 40000 | 40000 | 40000 | 480000 | |
| 95000 | 95000 | 95000 | 95000 | 95000 | 95000 | 1140000 | 1140000 |
| 0 | 0 | 0 | 0 | 0 | 0 | 50000 | |
| 0 | 0 | 0 | 25000 | 0 | 0 | 30000 | |
| 0 | 0 | 0 | 25000 | 0 | 0 | 80000 | 80000 |
| 2000 | 2000 | 2000 | 2000 | 2000 | 2000 | 26000 | |
| 2000 | 2000 | 2000 | 2000 | 2000 | 2000 | 26000 | 26000 |
| 28000 | 28000 | 28000 | 28000 | 28000 | 28000 | 336000 | |
| 16000 | 16000 | 16000 | 16000 | 16000 | 16000 | 192000 | |
| 2400 | 2400 | 2400 | 2400 | 2400 | 2400 | 28800 | |
| 4500 | 4500 | 4500 | 4500 | 4500 | 4500 | 54000 | |
| 50900 | 50900 | 50900 | 50900 | 50900 | 50900 | 610800 | 610800 |
| 0 | 500 | 0 | 0 | 500 | 0 | 2000 | |
| 0 | 0 | 200 | 0 | 0 | 700 | 2500 | |
| 600 | 600 | 600 | 600 | 600 | 600 | 7200 | |
| 20000 | 20000 | 20000 | 20000 | 20000 | 20000 | 240000 | |
| 300 | 300 | 300 | 300 | 300 | 300 | 3600 | |
| 20900 | 21400 | 21100 | 20900 | 21400 | 21600 | 255300 | 255300 |
| 400 | 400 | 400 | 400 | 400 | 400 | 7300 | |
| 100 | 100 | 100 | 100 | 100 | 100 | 1200 | |
| 600 | 600 | 600 | 600 | 600 | 600 | 7200 | |
| 90 | 90 | 90 | 90 | 90 | 90 | 1080 | |
| 200 | 200 | 200 | 200 | 200 | 200 | 2000 | |
| 17000 | 17000 | 17000 | 17000 | 17000 | 17000 | 204000 | |
| 85 | 85 | 85 | 85 | 85 | 85 | 1020 | |
| 0 | 325 | 0 | 0 | 325 | 0 | 1300 | |
| 100 | 100 | 100 | 100 | 100 | 100 | 1200 | |
| 18575 | 18900 | 18575 | 18575 | 18900 | 18575 | 226300 | 226300 |
| 92375 | 93200 | 92575 | 117375 | 93200 | 93075 | 1198400 | 1198400 |
| Jul | Aug | Sep | Oct | Nov | Dec | Year | |
| 2625 | 1800 | 2425 | -22375 | 1800 | 1925 | -58400 | -58400 |
| 11600 | -8975 | -7175 | -4750 | -27125 | -25325 | | |
| ?5000 | 95000 | 95000 | 95000 | 95000 | 95000 | 1140000 | |
| 92375 | 93200 | 92575 | 117375 | 93200 | 93075 | 1198400 | |
| -8975 | -7175 | -4750 | -27125 | -25325 | -23400 | | |

131

With the exception of the bank Balance B/F, which can just be invented, the others should be linked to their adjacent months as follows.

Put these links and Balance B/F figure into CASH01 :

| Row | Heading | Jan | Dec |
|---|---|---|---|
| 7 | From sales – Widgets Mk1 | C7 | |
| 8 | From sales – Widgets Mk2 | C8 | |
| 24 | Parts for Widgets Mk1 | | L24 |
| 25 | Parts for Widgets Mk2 | | L25 |
| 26 | Diesel fuel (Deliveries) | C26 | |
| 61 | Balance B/F | 35000 | |

★CASH01 to enter the links yourself, or ★CASH01P for the preprepared version.

Figure 7.3 (see page 130) shows how the cash flow forecast looks now.

# Graphs and key indicators
■   ■   ■

One of the more obvious features of the complete budget layout in Figure 7.2, and the cash flow layout in Figure 7.3, is that they both have a lot of numbers on them! You will find that you have to study them for quite a while – especially the cash flow – to get an understanding of what is going on. More significantly, once changes start to be made, and different scenarios are being tested, it really isn't possible to absorb all of the relevant effects that are necessary for an overall view.

> When considering a plan for capital investment it may be necessary to determine its effect on cash flow – will borrowing be necessary, if so, how much and when – for a variety of proposals.

There are two main ways of overcoming this difficulty, *graphs* and *key indicators*. With both of them, most advantage is obtained by minimising the amount of information presented, and ensuring that it is strictly appropriate to the view you are after.

Both are extremely quick and easy to set up, and whilst there will, without doubt, be a number of 'standard' graphs and key indicators that you will want to retain in your spreadsheet, many will only be set up temporarily for a specific purpose, and will be discarded once the job is done.

A *key indicator* is simply the drawing out or highlighting of some feature of special interest. For example, when considering a plan for capital investment it may be necessary to determine its effect on cash flow – will borrowing be necessary, if so, how much and when – for a variety of proposals. To see these on the cash flow, it will be necessary, for each proposal, to scan along the closing balance row and find the lowest figure. Have a quick look for the minimum balance on Figure 7.3 (★**CASH01**).

A 'minimum balance' key indicator makes it much easier to immediately see the effect of different proposals, here are examples of two ways of providing them:

1  In B68 use the MINimum function like this:

**MIN(B64.M64)**

2  In row 66, column B, use this function:

**IF(B64=$B$68),"Min","")**

and copy to December. This will compare the minimum value obtained above, with each month's closing balance, and display **Min** where they are the same.

133

The result of both of these is shown in Figure 7.4 (★**CASH01**) below, which is the lower portion of **CASH01**. The Minimum balance is shown at B68 (it could of course be put anywhere on the spreadsheet), and 'Min' is displayed in row 66 below where the minimum occurs.

### Figure 7.4 (★CASH01)  Minimum balance key indicator

*Graphs* are most useful for displaying trends and comparisons, but be careful not to put too much information on one chart, or it will become as difficult to interpret as rows of figures. It can sometimes be useful to also include a key indicator on a chart.

Figure 7.5 (see page 134), which is a chart on the cash flow spreadsheet, shows the closing balance and net cash flow for each month graphically.

**Figure 7.5 (✱CASH01 – chart 1)**

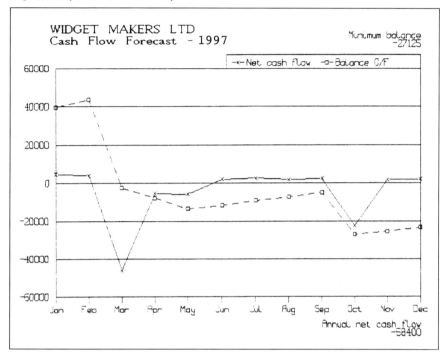

It also displays the minimum closing bank balance as a figure at the top right, and the annual net cash flow at the bottom right.

# Key ratios
■ ■ ■

A key ratio is strictly, and usually, the quotient (result) of one figure divided by another, but the term can be used for any arithmetic operation carried out on a number of figures to produce a single meaningful result.

For example, monthly sales can be divided by the number of people employed to give: £ *Sales per employee*, usually written as:

### £ Sales/Employee

Another example, net profit divided by widget sales volumes gives:

### £ Net Profit/Widget

And some more:

**Direct cost/sale**
**Direct costs/direct employee**
**Direct costs/total costs**
**Gross profit/employee**
**Gross profit/sale**
**Net profit/employee**
**Net profit/sale**
**Overhead cost/sale**
**Overhead costs/employee**
**Overhead costs/direct costs**
**Overhead costs/total costs**
**Sales/direct employee**
**Total cost/sale**

> Graphs, key indicators, key ratios, percentages and averages are the basic analytical tools of the budget forecaster's trade. But they should only be used when necessary, and often this will be for some specific task after which they can be discarded.

Key ratios may also be presented as percentage values, for example:

135

**Gross profit as a percentage of sales.**
**Net profit as a percentage of sales.**

Percentage values are sometimes easier to relate to than the raw ratio figure.

**Averages** can also provide figures that will help to isolate and highlight significant features of a company's budget. They are most useful for smoothing the peaks and troughs that would otherwise obscure a clear view of performance trends. For example:

■ average cash flow;
■ average variable direct costs;
■ average sales;
■ average total cost;
■ average overheads.

Graphs, key indicators, key ratios, percentages and averages are the basic analytical tools of the budget forecaster's trade. But they should only be used when necessary, and often this will be for some specific task after which they can be discarded. It is very easy indeed to create large numbers of diverse analytical figures and ratios on a spreadsheet, but if there are too many, their significance is likely to be lost in the crowd, and instead of clarifying the spreadsheet, it will become even harder to interpret.

## Save copy

Now that all of the data has been entered in your spreadsheet models, it would be wise to make another 'save' copy, so that you have them to return to later if necessary. Give this stage the file extension **.SV2** so that .SV1 you made at the beginning of this chapter is not overwritten.

## Summary

In this chapter:

- the first estimates of sales and budget forecast figures have been entered into the spreadsheet models;

- the rationale behind the way in which costs have been spread has been examined;

- the cash flow forecast has been adjusted with 'intelligent dummy' figures to generate a meaningful view of the year;

- the use of graphs and key indicators has been introduced;

- key ratios and other analytical tools and figures provide valuable insight, but *only* if used sparingly and with caution;

- save copies were made at significant stages, .SV1 for the basic frameworks, and .SV2 once all of the figures had been entered;

The complete budget forecast is now assembled, and is ready for closer examination and any necessary adjustments – the reiteration process.

Reiteration of the budgeting process is extremely important; it not only reduces the likelihood of errors going unnoticed, but also provides opportunities to spot many more significant features that might otherwise be lost amongst the plethora of figures in the sales, budget and cash flow forecasts.

# 8
■ ■ ■

# Causes and effects

The reiteration process ■   139

Practical aspects of examining effects ■

Simple cause and effect ■

Where to start – with the cause or the effect? ■

Gross profitability of each product ■

N ow that figures have been put into the sales and budget forecast frame-works, and the cash flow forecast has been linked to them, if the fore-casters and their colleagues are completely satisfied with what they show, then no further work on them is necessary and they can be put to work immediately for budget allocation and operational monitoring. But, usually life isn't like that!

> Budget forecasting is, far more often than not, a process of adjustment and refinement, of reiteration through the models until everyone is satisfied – for now – that what they show represents the most realistic forecast of reality they can muster.

Budget forecasting is, far more often than not, a process of adjustment and refinement, of reiteration through the models until everyone is satisfied – for now – that what they show represents the most realistic forecast of reality they can muster. And of course, this reiteration is what spreadsheet-based forecasts are so good at, partly because they will recalculate changes so quickly, but more significantly because the relationships between all of the elements, the cause and effects, are intrinsically built into the models.

In this chapter the practical aspects of reiteration are considered, simple cause and effect are discussed, and examples of them are illus-trated.

140

---

**Note for users of the illustration disc** – because the illustration disc models are now complete, you can use them to try any of the examples and techniques described. Although you will be making the data changes to the model yourself, the charts shown in the book are already set up in them.

**Remember** – all of the original models are still on the floppy disc you were sup-plied with, and copies of these can be transferred to your hard disc to return you to this point.

---

## The reiteration process
■ ■ ■

In the world of budget forecasting, reiteration on the scale that will be employed by us was unheard of before computers were put to the task. It simply wasn't practicable, and this was most unfortunate, because even a budget that has been polished and refined through many iterative loops still won't be absolutely right. So, what chance did a single run through, with perhaps one or two minor retrospective modifications stand!

Reiteration of the budgeting process is extremely important; it not only reduces the likelihood of errors going unnoticed, but also provides opportunities to spot many more significant features that might otherwise be lost amongst the plethora of figures in the sales, budget and cash flow forecasts. This highlights the importance of the sparing use of key indicators, ratios and graphs with only essential detail on them.

Because there are so many figures and factors that could be considered, it is best to focus on just one or two at a time. Then change some values, see the effect and change again if necessary ... and so on. The means of focus might be nothing more than keeping an eye on the appropriate figures, or may require that some key indicators, key ratios, or a graph are set up. These can be either temporary, or established as permanent features. If you're not sure whether any of them will be needed again, assume that they will be, and put them in a suitable place and form. If you are certain that an indicator won't be needed again, then it can be put into any convenient cell, and deleted once the job is done.

# Practical aspects of examining effects

■ ■ ■

The way in which changes are made, and their influence is examined, depends upon whether the cause and effect are on the same spreadsheet model, and if they are not, upon some technical features of your computer and spreadsheet type.

Clearly, if the cause and effect are on the same spreadsheet, then the change can be made and the impact seen immediately.

If, however cause and effect are on separate, but linked spreadsheet models, as those for Widget Makers Ltd often will be, then the options, in order of preference, are:

1 Load all of the spreadsheet models into memory, then switch between them as required.
2 If only one model can be in memory at any one time, and if the spreadsheet type will allow, refresh the links to models on the disc that are dependent upon the changes.
3 If only one model can be in memory at any one time, and the spreadsheet type does not provide for link refreshment to files on the disc, then each model must be loaded in turn, recalculated and saved back to the disc. *This must be done in order of dependency*, for Widget Makers Ltd the order is:

First – SALES01
Second – BUDG01
Third – CASH01

If you are not sure what facilities you have, check with your spreadsheet supplier.

# Simple cause and effect
■ ■ ■

There is no better way than 'playing' with a spreadsheet model to develop an understanding of the relationship between cause and effect in financial budgets. Although the relationships can get extremely complex when many factors are involved – to the point where an average brain simply cannot perceive their interaction as a whole – the spreadsheet model will still unswervingly supply the correct end result. Whilst it may be very frustrating to not understand fully why, it is at least satisfying to be sure of the 'what'. Examples of some more complex relationships will be explored in Chapter 10.

For now we will concentrate on simple relationships. Firstly by discussing a range of 'causes', and then by trying them out on the spreadsheet models for Widget Makers Ltd. The cause factors that will be looked at are:

### 1 Sales

- Sales volumes
- Sales price

### 2 Cost

- Capital expenditure
- Start up expenditure
- Variable direct costs
- Constant direct costs
- Overheads

### 3 Timing

- Cash payment timing
- Sales receipt timing
- General.

There is a summary table of causes and their effects at the end of this section.

# 1 Sales factors

## Sales volumes

Selling more means bigger profits and a larger bank balance? Possibly, but the converse may also be true. 'Bigger profits' assumes that every item sold makes a profit, but if sufficient of them don't, then selling more will create a larger loss. 'Larger bank balance' also assumes profitability, but, more significantly, requires a lot of qualification if there is continual sales growth. The detailed effect of volume growth on cash flow depends upon several factors including, net profit and the nature, value and timing of variable direct costs. It is quite possible, and often all too probable, for a company to run out of cash when business is booming. The subject is discussed in detail in Chapter 10.

However, assuming profitable sales and no sales volume growth, then it is reasonable to assume:

| *Cause* | *Effect* |
|---------|----------|
| Higher sales volumes | Higher gross profit |
| | Higher net profit |
| | More cash in the bank – probably |

143

## Sales price

In any given stable situation, and ignoring any marketing and sales factors such as competition, for the purpose of budget forecasts it is safe to assume:

| *Cause* | *Effect* |
|---------|----------|
| Higher sales price | Higher gross profit |
| | Higher net profit |
| | More cash in the bank |

# 2 Cost factors

## Capital expenditure

There are several ways of viewing capital expenditure, and of dealing with it in a budget forecast and allocation. A thorough discussion of the subject would fill a book in itself, and, in any event, is unnecessary for budgeting so long as a consistent, or at least widely understood, policy is adopted.

Some questions a forecaster needs answers to are the following. The responses given are for Widget Makers Ltd:

(a) Is capital expenditure to be shown in the budget?*                                  Yes
(b) Is the expenditure a cost on gross or net profit?                                    No
(c) Are fixed assets to be included in the budget?                                       No
(d) Is depreciation of assets to be included in the budget?                              No
(e) Is the interest on any capital financing to be included in the budget?   No

* If a cash flow will be associated with the budget, and the answer to question (b) is 'Yes', then capital expenditure must appear in both the budget and the cash flow forecasts.

If a cash flow will be associated with the budget, and the answer to question (b) is 'No', it *must* at least appear in the cash flow forecast, but may also be in both. For Widget Makers Ltd it is shown in both, although it does not figure in profitability calculations.

A final point on capital expenditure. It may well be an investment, in a new machine for instance, that will improve productivity and reduce costs. Clearly this effect needs to be accounted for in the budget, but it isn't necessary for just that reason to include the capital expenditure itself in the budget forecast or allocation.

However, it is shown in Widget Maker's budget, but does not affect profit figures, hence:

| Cause | Effect |
|---|---|
| Capital expenditure | Less cash in the bank |

## Start up expenditure

In some ways, start up expenditure begs the same questions as those for capital expenditure. If the start up cost is for a capital item, then it will be categorised and treated as such. Assuming that it isn't capital expenditure, a forecaster may like to consider the following points. Again the responses shown are those that apply to Widget Makers Ltd:

(a) Is start up expenditure to be included in the budget?*                               Yes
(b) Is the expenditure a cost on gross or net profit?                                     No
(c) Is the interest on any start up financing to be included in the budget?   No

* The comments made for (b) in capital expenditure also apply to start up costs.

The points made for capital investment are also true for start up expenditure. A start up cost is often an investment in a new product, and if account is to be taken of it in profitability, then it must either be regarded as an overhead, or as a direct cost of the new product, even if the product doesn't yet exist.

Widget Makers Ltd have decided not to include the design and development costs in the profitability shown on the budget, although it does appear there as well as on the cash flow forecast. Thus:

*Cause*                          *Effect*
Start up expenditure             Less cash in the bank

> **Note:** Start up costs, together with other items not included anywhere in the example budget for Widget Makers Ltd – such as loan interest and depreciation – *will* figure in profit calculations in the company's annual audited accounts. They are excluded here for the sake of simplicity.

## Variable direct costs

These are costs directly associated with the product, and thus directly affect gross profit, and hence, also net profit.

Characteristics of *variable* direct costs that are of most interest to a forecaster include their:

- arithmetic relationship to volume;
- proportion of total (variable + constant) direct costs;
- proportion to total (direct + overhead) costs;
- timing with respect to payment for them;
- timing with respect to sales receipts;
- magnitude with respect to gross and net profit.

As can be judged by this list, variable direct costs are at the root of a number of fairly complex relationships, and these will be looked at more closely in Chapter 10. Simplistically though:

*Cause*                          *Effect*
Higher variable direct cost      Lower gross profit
                                 Lower net profit
                                 Less cash in the bank

The converse of these is true for lower variable direct costs.

### Constant direct costs

These costs are directly associated with the product and will affect both gross and net profit.

Like all costs, the timing of payment for them is important, and in the case of constant direct costs, their proportion of both total direct costs and total overall costs. Their effects are the same as constant direct costs, but in a less dynamic way because they are not influenced by volumes:

| *Cause* | *Effect* |
|---|---|
| Higher constant direct costs | Lower gross profit |
| | Lower net profit |
| | Less cash in the bank |

The converse of these is true for lower constant direct costs.

### Overheads

These are the costs not directly associated with the product, they will therefore not affect gross profit. Their proportion of the total costs is important during volume growth, as is the timing of the payment for them on cash flow:

| *Cause* | *Effect* |
|---|---|
| Higher overhead costs | Lower net profit |
| | Less cash in the bank |

The converse of these is true for lower overhead costs.

## 3 Timing factors

### Cash payment timing

In the calculation of profit, it is *what* and 'how much' that are important, whereas cash flow is all about *when* and 'how much'.

There is, however, a link from cash flow back to profit. If money is borrowed, whether as a formal loan, a bank overdraft, or any other kind of financing arrangement that incurs a charge, then that charge will figure in the calculation of profit. As with all other aspects of financial control, spreadsheets are ideally suited to their calculation and feeding back into the profit figures. However, interest charges have not been included in the example of Widget Makers Ltd and thus payment timing affects only cash flow:

| *Cause* | *Effect* |
|---|---|
| Earlier cash payment | Less cash in the bank |
| Later cash payment | More cash in the bank |

## Sales receipt timing

All of the points made for cash payment timing are also true for sales receipt timing, but their effects are precisely the converse:

| Cause | Effect |
|---|---|
| Earlier sales receipt | More cash in the bank |
| Later sales receipt | Less cash in the bank |

## General

Whilst the simple impact of cash flow timing is reflected only by the bank balance, and in the profit if interest charges are incurred, poor cash flow has very much wider implications, especially during volume growth. In Chapter 10 it will be shown how a fundamentally profitable business with increasing sales can run into cash availability problems, which will at best inhibit their growth, or at worst make their survival dependent upon the consideration and forbearance of their source of finance – the bank perhaps.

## Cause and effect summary

Figure 8.1 (see page 148) summarises simple cause and effect, ↑ means higher or better, ↓ means lower or worse. A blank entry indicates that in simple relationships there is no impact.

Note from the table that a change to *gross* profit always affects *net* profit.

# Where to start – with the cause or the effect?
■ ■ ■

This heading suggests that there are only two ways of deciding what changes to make in the reiterative process – looking first at the *causes* and working out the *effect* of a change, or looking first at the *effect* and working out what changes need to be made to the *causes* to achieve a desired result.

There is, however, a third method – it's called 'suck it and see!', or 'trial and error'. In practice this third method is probably used more than any other, and again (I

> It is important to first have an understanding of what is happening in the forecasts when figures are changed and the outcome checked in this way.

know I keep on saying it), spreadsheets are ideally suited to it. *But*, it is important to first have an understanding of what is happening in the forecasts when figures are changed and the outcome checked in this way. *Then*, you are properly equipped to use trial and error as much as you like.

## Figure 8.1 Summary table of simple cause and effect

| CAUSES | Gross Profit | Net Profit | Cash Flow | |
|---|---|---|---|---|
| **Sales factors** | | | | |
| Sales volume higher | ↑ | ↑ | ↑ | |
| Sales volume lower | ↓ | ↓ | ↑ | |
| Sales volume increasing | ↑ | ↑ | O | See Chapter 10 |
| Sales volume decreasing | ↓ | ↓ | O | See Chapter 10 |
| Sales price up | ↑ | ↑ | ↑ | |
| Sales price down | ↓ | ↓ | ↓ | |
| **Cost factors** | | | | |
| Capital cost | * | * | ↓ | *Subject to company policy |
| Start up cost | | | ↓ | |
| Variable direct cost up | ↓ | ↓ | ↓ | |
| Variable direct cost down | ↑ | ↑ | ↑ | |
| Constant direct cost up | ↓ | ↓ | ↓ | |
| Constant direct cost down | ↑ | ↑ | ↑ | |
| Overheads up | | ↓ | ↓ | |
| Overheads down | | ↑ | ↑ | |
| **Timing factors** | | | | |
| Cash payment earlier | | | ↓ | |
| Cash payment later | | | ↑ | |
| Sales receipt earlier | | | ↑ | |
| Sales receipt later | | | ↓ | |

Above the Effects columns: ............... EFFECTS ...............

In this section, the two formal methods will be looked at with an example of each, using two of the simple cause and effects discussed earlier. Trial and error will also feature in both.

These will be followed by less detailed examples of the rest of the simple cause and effects. The section will also provide practical illustrations of the use of key indicators, ratios and graphs.

# Method 1

The desired *effect* is known. What changes to causes are needed?

## Example 1 – Improving gross profit

In this example, calculation of gross profit is added to the budget forecast, and the changes necessary to improve it are examined and tested.

For use later on, net profit calculations will also be added.

> *Reminder:*
> **Gross profit = Revenue – Direct costs**
> **Net profit = Revenue – (Direct costs + Overhead costs)**

The first task is to set up some key indicators – in this case views of gross profit and net profit. A graphical representation will also be useful.

Profitability can be calculated on the budget forecast, and we are assuming that Widget Makers Ltd choose to exclude capital and start up costs from it.

The new row headings and formulae for the budget forecast in Figure 8.2 (see below) show the calculation of gross and net profit, and how both are also expressed as percentage of sales. Only column B (Jan) is illustrated, but the formulae should be copied through to column M (Dec). The formulae in column N show how the full year's revenue and costs are used to calculate annual profit percentages.

### Figure 8.2 (*BUDG01) Calculation of gross and net profit

```
   |          A              ||    B      ||   N    ||
71
72
73          PROFITABILITY
74  (Excluding capital and start up)
75
76  Revenue from sales        B15         IF(SUM(B76:M76)<>0,SUM(B76:M76),"")
77  Direct costs              B42+B51     IF(SUM(B77:M77)<>0,SUM(B77:M77),"")
78         Gross profit  B76-B77          IF(SUM(B78:M78)<>0,SUM(B78:M78),"")
79       as % of sales B78/B76*100        N78/N76*100
80
81  Overhead costs            B64         IF(SUM(B81:M81)<>0,SUM(B81:M81),"")
82  Total costs               B77+B81     IF(SUM(B82:M82)<>0,SUM(B82:M82),"")
83           Net profit B76-B82           IF(SUM(B83:M83)<>0,SUM(B83:M83),"")
84       as % of sales B83/B76*100        N83/N76*100
```

Figure 8.3 (see page 150) shows what the profit figures look like for the forecast as it was left in the last chapter. Focus on the percentage of sales figures.

> **Note:** Because the addition of the profit calculation rows is a significant change, make another 'save' copy with the extension .SV3.

Gross profit is 24 per cent of sales, but suppose that a figure of nearer 30 per cent is wanted by December. What changes are necessary to achieve that objective?

150

## Figure 8.3 (∗BUDG01) Gross and net profit

| | A | B | C | D | E | F | G | H | I | J | K | L | M | N |
|---|---|---|---|---|---|---|---|---|---|---|---|---|---|---|
| | | Jan | Feb | Mar | Apr | May | Jun | Jul | Aug | Sep | Oct | Nov | Dec | Year |
| 73 | PROFITABILITY | | | | | | | | | | | | | |
| 74 | (Excluding capital and start up) | | | | | | | | | | | | | |
| 75 | | | | | | | | | | | | | | |
| 76 | Revenue from sales | 95000 | 95000 | 95000 | 95000 | 95000 | 95000 | 95000 | 95000 | 95000 | 95000 | 95000 | 95000 | 1140000 |
| 77 | Direct costs | 71800 | 72300 | 72700 | 71800 | 72300 | 72500 | 71800 | 72300 | 72000 | 71800 | 72300 | 72500 | 866100 |
| 78 | Gross profit | 23200 | 22700 | 22300 | 23200 | 22700 | 22500 | 23200 | 22700 | 23000 | 23200 | 22700 | 22500 | 273900 |
| 79 | as % of sales | 24 | 24 | 23 | 24 | 24 | 24 | 24 | 24 | 24 | 24 | 24 | 24 | 24 |
| 80 | | | | | | | | | | | | | | |
| 81 | Overhead costs | 18575 | 18700 | 18575 | 18575 | 21400 | 18575 | 18575 | 18900 | 18575 | 18575 | 18900 | 18575 | 226300 |
| 82 | Total costs | 90375 | 91000 | 91075 | 90375 | 93700 | 91075 | 90375 | 91200 | 90575 | 90375 | 91200 | 91075 | 1092400 |
| 83 | Net profit | 4625 | 4000 | 3925 | 4625 | 1300 | 3925 | 4625 | 3800 | 4425 | 4625 | 3800 | 3925 | 47600 |
| 84 | as % of sales | 5 | 4 | 4 | 5 | 1 | 4 | 5 | 4 | 5 | 5 | 4 | 4 | 4 |

*Now then* – if you *really* must, you can skip over this next bit and pick up again at 'Trial and error'. But if you do, why not try coming back here afterwards.

The ratio is *gross profit/sales*, and so to improve the figure, either the gross profit must be increased by a greater proportion than the sales that produce it, or sales must be reduced by a smaller proportion than their effect on gross profit.

On the assumption that we have no wish to reduce sales, the solution will be found by endeavouring to increase gross profit whilst maintaining sales at the current level.

*Gross profit is revenue* – *direct costs*, thus, if sales revenue is to be held constant, direct costs must be addressed to improve gross profit.

*Direct costs* consist of *variable directs* and *constant directs*, and so reducing either of them will have the desired effect, but it would be best to concentrate first on whichever of them will have the most significant impact on the total direct costs.

A glance at the budget forecast will show that variable direct costs are £51,000/month, and constant direct costs are on average about £21,000/month.

**Figure 8.4 (∗BUDG01 – Chart DIRECTCOST)**
**Variable and constant direct costs**

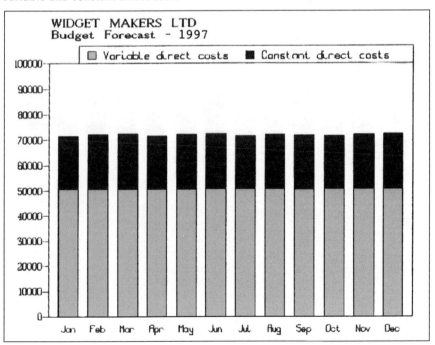

Figure 8.4 (see page 151) is a bar chart of the direct costs. Using a stacked bar like this makes it very easy to see the total of two sets of figures, and the proportion of one to the other.

Variable direct costs are about 71 per cent (50,000/70,000) of the total direct costs, and constant directs, therefore, some 29 per cent.

Clearly then, on average constant direct costs of £21,000/month, and variable direct costs of £51,000/month, a 10 per cent reduction of both would bring monthly reductions of £2,100 and £5,100 respectively. Furthermore, although for this exercise sales volumes are being held constant, it is worth bearing in mind that if sales volumes do increase, the savings from reduced constant direct costs will be unaffected, *whilst the savings on variable direct costs will also increase*.

This can be illustrated by *temporarily* increasing sales volumes for Widgets Mk1 and Mk2 by 20 per cent, to 240/month and 120/month respectively, and looking again at the chart of direct costs.

We can see in Figure 8.5 (below) that whilst the constant direct costs are of course unchanged, variable direct costs have increased and now represent about 75 per cent (60,000/80,000) of the total.

**Figure 8.5 (∗BUDG01 – Chart DIRECTCOST)**
**Variable costs increased**

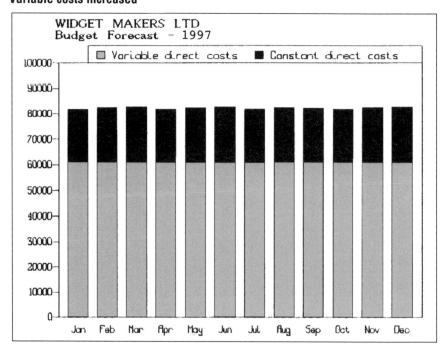

**Note:** The change in sales volumes above was only temporary, they should now be set back to 200/month for Widgets Mk1, and 100/month for Widgets Mk2.

Therefore, the most productive costs to address initially are the variable directs, and of these, by far the greater portion of variable direct costs are for the widget parts, their annual totals are £336,000 for the Mk1, and £192,000 for the Mk2.

OK – so by how much should the variable direct costs be reduced to increase gross profit from 24 per cent to 30 per cent by December? The formulae isn't especially simple, particularly as in practice the solution is likely to be a gradual change, rather than a single one. It would, therefore, be quite in order, and certainly quicker, to now use trial and error on the widget parts costs to achieve a gross profit of 30 per cent by December.

For those who are interested, here is a means of calculating what percentage reduction of variable direct costs is needed to increase gross profit from 24 per cent to 30 per cent as a single change.

**Figure 8.5a  Calculation of variable direct costs necessary to achieve a 30 per cent gross profit**

For this formulae:

$P$ = Percentage gross profit (%)
$SR$ = Sales revenue (£140,000)
$CD$ = Constant direct costs (£255,300)
$VD$ = Variable direct costs (£610,800 initially)

i) $P = \dfrac{SR - CD + VD}{SR} \times 100$

ii) $\dfrac{P \times SR}{100} = SR - CD + VD$

iii) $CD + VD = SR - \dfrac{P \times SR}{100}$

iv) $VD = SR - \dfrac{P \times SR}{100} - CD$

Substituting values for 30% gross profit:

v) $VD = 1,140,000 - \dfrac{30 \times 1,140,000}{100} - 255,300$

vi) $VD = 1,140,000 - 342,000 - 255,300$

vii) $VD = 542,700$

which is a variable direct costs reduction of 610,800 – 542,700 = **£68,100** or **11.15%**

The reduction of **total** variable costs necessary, including constants of £255,300, is (255,300 + 610,800) – (255,300 + 542,700) = **£68,100** or **7.9%**

## Trial and error

To work out what changes are needed to achieve a 30 per cent of sales gross profit by trial and error, and to introduce a smooth progression of reducing variable direct costs, it is simply a matter of replacing the figure for widget parts costs with a reducing formulae from February onwards, checking the result, and trying again if necessary. To make it clearer, we'll go through the process once.

Let's suppose that we manage to find an alternative supplier of widget parts, who agrees to reduce the prices by 1.5 per cent, month on month, throughout the year. To examine the impact of this, enter the formulae **B29–(B29*.015)** in C29 of BUDG01, and copy it down to C30 and across to column M (Dec). Figure 8.6 (below) shows the formulae in column C.

Figure 8.7 (opposite) shows the effect of the price reduction on the cost of parts, and the total variable direct costs, throughout the year.

The total variable direct costs have been reduced from £610,800 to £569,346, a reduction of £41,454 or 6.8 per cent.

### Figure 8.6 (*BUDG01) Formulae for reducing widget parts costs

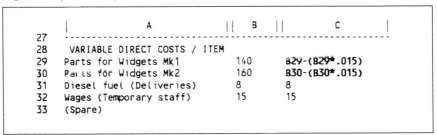

**Figure 8.7 (★BUDG01) Reducing widget parts cost**

| | A | B | C | D | E | F | G | H | I | J | K | L | M | N |
|---|---|---|---|---|---|---|---|---|---|---|---|---|---|---|
| 28 | VARIABLE DIRECT COSTS / ITEM | | | | | | | | | | | | | |
| 29 | Parts for Widgets Mk1 | 140 | 138 | 136 | 134 | 132 | 130 | 128 | 126 | 124 | 122 | 120 | 119 | |
| 30 | Parts for Widgets Mk2 | 160 | 158 | 155 | 153 | 151 | 148 | 146 | 144 | 142 | 140 | 138 | 135 | |
| 31 | Diesel fuel (Deliveries) | 8 | 8 | 8 | 8 | 8 | 8 | 8 | 8 | 8 | 8 | 8 | 8 | |
| 32 | Wages (Temporary staff) | 15 | 15 | 15 | 15 | 15 | 15 | 15 | 15 | 15 | 15 | 15 | 15 | |
| 33 | (Spare) | | | | | | | | | | | | | |
| 34 | | | | | | | | | | | | | | |
| 35 | VARIABLE DIRECT COSTS | | | | | | | | | | | | | |
| 36 | (Vol x Cost / Item) | | | | | | | | | | | | | |
| 37 | Parts for Widgets Mk1 | 28000 | 27580 | 27166 | 26759 | 26357 | 25962 | 25573 | 25189 | 24811 | 24439 | 24072 | 23711 | 309620 |
| 38 | Parts for Widgets Mk2 | 16000 | 15760 | 15524 | 15291 | 15061 | 14835 | 14613 | 14394 | 14178 | 13965 | 13756 | 13549 | 176926 |
| 39 | Diesel fuel (Deliveries) | 2400 | 2400 | 2400 | 2400 | 2400 | 2400 | 2400 | 2400 | 2400 | 2400 | 2400 | 2400 | 28800 |
| 40 | Wages (Temporary staff) | 4500 | 4500 | 4500 | 4500 | 4500 | 4500 | 4500 | 4500 | 4500 | 4500 | 4500 | 4500 | 54000 |
| 41 | (Spare) | | | | | | | | | | | | | |
| 42 | Total (C) | 50900 | 50240 | 49590 | 48950 | 48319 | 47698 | 47086 | 46483 | 45889 | 45304 | 44728 | 44161 | 569346 |

The easiest way to view the gross profit is on a graph, Figure 8.8 (below) shows the reducing variable direct costs together with the rising gross profit as a percentage on sales.

**Figure 8.8 (∗BUDG01 – Chart VARGOSS)**
**Decreasing variable direct costs and increasing gross profit**

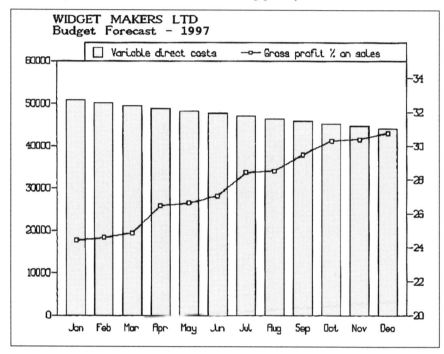

We can see that monthly gross profit is up to about 31 per cent by December; slightly exceeding the target we set ourselves of 30 per cent.

The 'waves' in the gross profit line are the underlying effect of the quarterly electricity and gas constant direct costs.

The next graph, in Figure 8.9 (opposite), shows the same gross profit line – on a different scale and also includes net profit, illustrating that the changes to gross profit also affect net profit.

Whereas net profit through the year before the change was about 4 per cent of sales (this can be seen in Figure 8.3), it is now rising to around 11 per cent by December.

Finally for this example, look at the effect these changes have had on cash flow. Compare Figure 8.10 (opposite) with Figure 7.5 (see page 134).

**Figure 8.9 (★BUDG01 – Chart %PROFIT)**
**Net profit rising with gross profit**

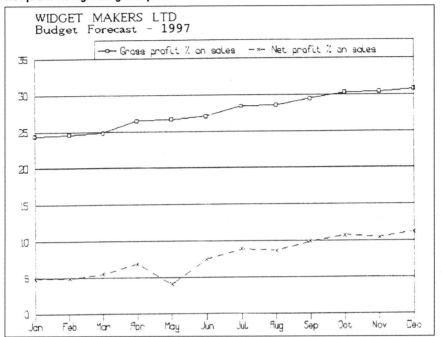

**Figure 8.10 (★CASH01 – Chart 1)**
**The effect of reducing variable direct costs on cash flow**

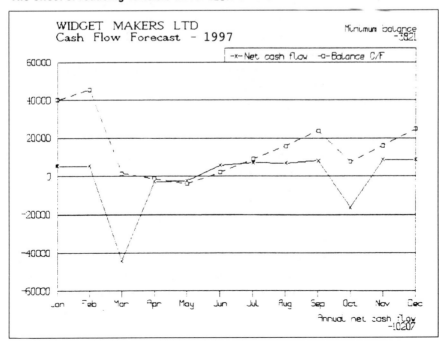

Net cash flow is now more positive. The minimum balance, which was –£27125 in October, is now only –£3821 in May, and there is a healthy balance of about £25,000 at the year end, instead of an overdraft of some –£25,000. Annual net cash flow has, of course, also improved by about £48,000.

If the overdraft represented a real bank account, and the interest due on borrowed money was being calculated in the cash flow model, then considerable savings from this would also be seen.

*This example is finished* – set the parts costs for Widgets Mk1 and Mk2 in the budget forecast (★**BUDG01**) back to £140 and £160 respectively for the whole year.

## Method 2

The change to a *cause* is known, what will be its effect?

### Example 2 – The effect of increased overheads

In this example, an overhead cost will rise half way through the year. The change will be entered into the budget forecast, and its effect examined.

*Reminder: Increased overheads reduce net profit and worsen cash flow.*

Suppose that Salaries (Management) are due to rise from £17,000/ month to £19,000/month from June onwards, what effect will this have?

Of course, it will only take a few seconds to find out by simply changing the numbers, but let's first just work out the sort of thing to expect. In any event, it's always a good idea to have a 'feel' for what might happen. If it doesn't, then either basic understanding is at fault, or the model is wrong – both of which are worth knowing about!

From the 'cause and effect' table (Figure 8.1), we know that increased overheads affect net profit and cash flow, but do not affect gross profit.

Figure 8.3 shows that net profit, as a percentage of sales, averages about 4 per cent throughout the year with the original figures that were entered. Thus an increase in overheads from June onwards will reduce net profit over the same period.

Now, change Salaries (Management) to £19,000 from June onwards in the budget forecast (★**BUDG01**). The effect on net profit can be seen in Figure 8.11 (opposite). The dip in May is due to a one-off expense on building maintenance of £2,900, but the continuing level of around 2.5 per cent from June is the impact of the salaries increase. Note also that gross profit is unchanged at about 24 per cent.

**Figure 8.11 (✶BUDG01 – Chart %PROFIT)**
**The effect of increased overheads on net profit**

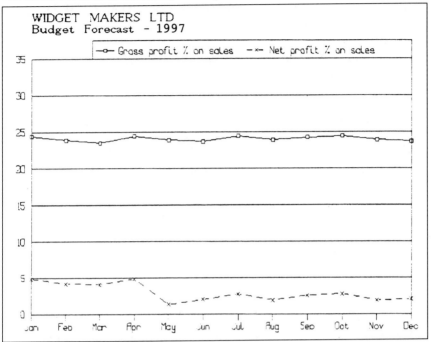

**Figure 8.12 (✶CASH01 – Chart 1)**
**The effect of increased overheads on cash flow**

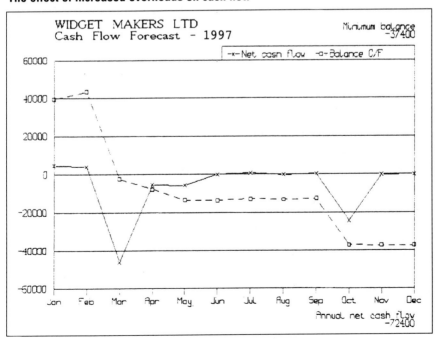

Overhead changes also affect cash flow, look back at Figure 8.12. When compared to Figure 7.5, which is based on the original figures, net cash flow is now barely positive during the summer. The annual figure has fallen to –£72,400, and the lowest balance has worsened to –£37,400 in December.

*This example is finished* – set Salaries(Management) in the budget forecast (★**BUDG01**) back to £17,000 from June to December.

# Further examples of cause and effect

### Example 3 – Single large expenses: capital and start up

In Widget Makers Ltd, neither capital nor start up expenses are included in profit calculations, but they do of course have a most significant affect on cash flow.

Figure 8.13 (opposite) shows the effect of removing the single payment capital expenses of:

160

£50,000 for factory machinery in March

£ 5,000 for office machinery in May

£25,000 for office machinery in October

This is a total of £80,000. Thus the annual net cash flow will be better by that amount compared with Figure 7.5, as will the closing bank balance at the year end.

*This example is finished* – restore capital expenditure in the budget forecast (★**BUDG01**)to:

| Factory machinery | Mar | 50,000 |
| Office machinery | May | 5,000 |
| " " | Oct | 25,000 |

### Example 4 – Increased constant direct costs

Constant direct costs affect gross profit, net profit and cash flow.

Suppose that Salaries (Widget production) increase to £22,000 from March onwards. Figure 8.14 (opposite) shows that both gross and net profits fall to an average of around 22 per cent and 2.5 per cent respectively. Though, net *profit* has become a *loss* in May due to the building maintenance expense of £2,900.

The effect on cash flow is shown in Figure 8.15 (see page 162). Note that the picture is similar to that created by increased overheads, this is because both are fixed changes to regular monthly payments.

**Figure 8.13 (★CASH01 – Chart 1)**
**The effect on cash flow when removing capital expenditure**

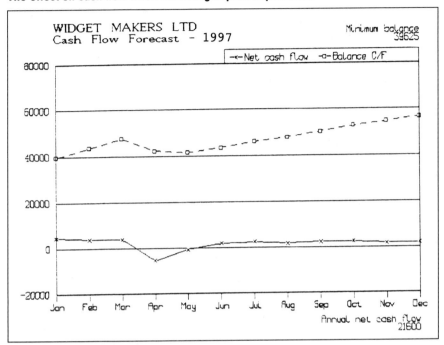

**Figure 8.14 (★BUDG01 – Chart %PROFIT)**
**The effect of increased constant directs on profit**

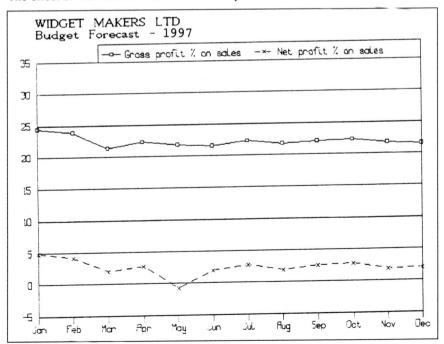

**Figure 8.15 (★CASH01 – Chart 1)**
**The effect of increased constant directs on cash flow**

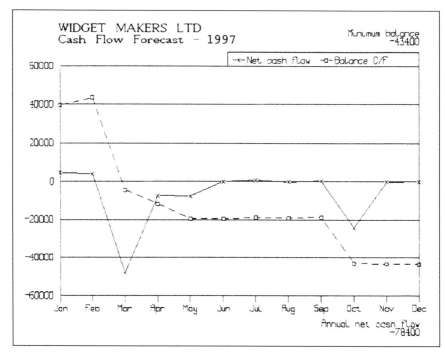

This example is finished – restore Salaries (Widget production) in the budget forecast (★**BUDG01**) to £22,000 from March onwards.

## Example 5 – Simple timing changes

By simple timing changes, I mean those that are just a shift of an expense, or revenue item, to another month. Timing changes during volume growth are more complex, and are dealt with in Chapter 10.

As the budget currently stands, there is a building maintenance expense of £2,900 in May. We'll examine what happens if, first of all, it is replanned for January, and secondly for December.

### 1 January

The single building maintenance expense has been moved in the budget forecast from May back to January. Figure 8.16 (opposite) shows that the gross profit line is unaffected (this is an overhead change), but that net profit is, as expected, reduced for January. *It is important to note that total net profit for the year is still the same*, because the total overhead expenditure has not altered.

**Figure 8.16 (★BUDG01 – Chart %PROFIT)**
**The effect of an earlier single overhead payment on profit**

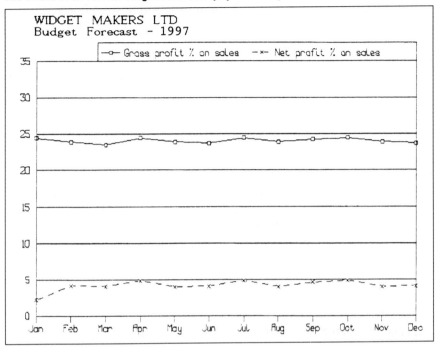

**Figure 8.17 (★CASH01 – Chart 1)**
**The effect of an earlier single overhead payment on cash flow**

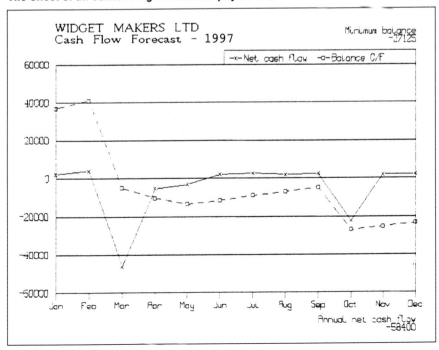

163

Figure 8.17 (see page 163) shows the impact on cash flow. Because the payment has been brought forward to a time when cash reserves were plentiful, the effect compared with Figure 7.5 is almost undetectable, and both minimum balance and annual net cash flow are exactly the same.

### 2 December

The single building maintenance expense of £2,900 has been moved forward to December. Again, save for a dip in net profit during that month, the overall net profit for the year is unchanged.

Cash flow, however, has not been affected a great deal, because the sum involved is not high compared with total expenditure, but it is noticeable. Figure 8.18 (below), shows that although the annual net cash flow is unaltered (the same total amount of cash has flowed through the business during the year), the minimum balance during the year has improved to –£24,625 in December compared with –£27,125 in October shown in Figure 7.5. This is because the minimum balance during October, seen in Figure 7.5, was partly due to the £2,900 building maintenance in May, which has now been moved beyond October to December.

### Figure 8.18 (★CASH01 – Chart 1)
### The effect of a later single overhead payment on cash flow

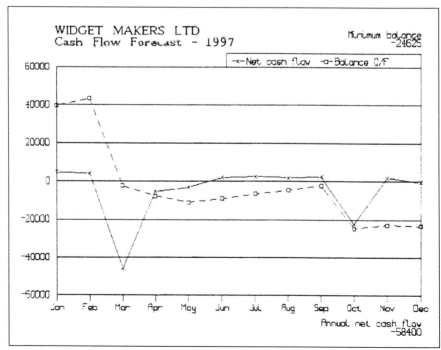

*This example is finished* – restore building maintenance of £2,900 in the budget forecast (★**BUDG01**) to May, and all other months to £400.

## Example 6 – All change!

In this final example of simple cause and effect, every change, except for removal of capital expenditure, that has been made in the previous examples will be incorporated. These are:

1  Reducing widget parts cost by 1.5 per cent from February. (Ex.1)
2  Salaries (Management) increased to £19,000 from June. (Ex.2)
3  Salaries (Widget production) increased to £22,000 from March. (Ex.4)
4  One timing change – building maintenance of £2,900 moved from May to December.

**Note:** Sales volume changes are dealt with in Chapter 10.

Figure 8.19 (below) and Figure 8.20 (see page 166) show the overall impact on profit and cash flow, respectively.

### Figure 8.19 (★BUDG01 – Chart %PROFIT)
### The effect of multiple changes on profit

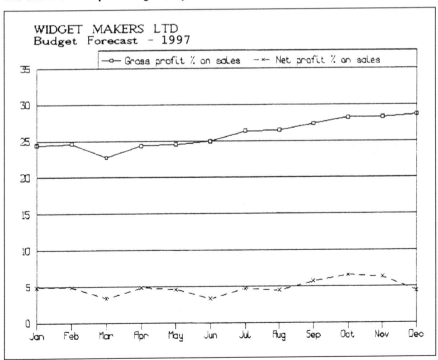

**Figure 8.20 (∗CASH01 – Chart 1)**
**The effect of multiple changes on cash flow**

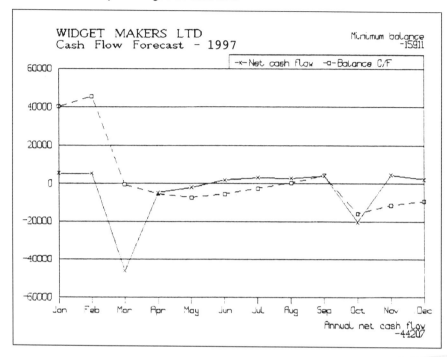

*This example is now finished* – you can either restore all of the changes for it individually, or otherwise make a copy of **BUDG01**.SV3 with the appropriate extension (.xls .wk1 .wks etc) to return to the latest model with the original data.

# Gross profitability of each product

The sale price and parts cost of each of the widget types are not the same, and because parts cost affects gross profit, they are likely to generate different gross profit of sales percentages.

The model does not separately identify constant direct costs for each product, they are bundled together, and so individual net profit figures cannot be calculated.

The new row headings and formulae for gross profit per product on the budget forecast are shown in Figure 8.21 (above, opposite). Only columns B and N are illustrated, the column B formulae must be copied through to column M (Dec).

## Figure 8.21 (*BUDG01) Calculation of gross profit per product

| | A | | B | | N | |
|---|---|---|---|---|---|---|
| 85 | | | | | | |
| 86 | BY PRODUCT | | | | | |
| 87 | Widgets Mk1 - gross profit | | B12-(B77/2) | | IF(SUM(B87:M87)<>0,SUM(B87:M87),"") | |
| 88 | as % of sales | | B87/B12*100 | | M87/N12*100 | |
| 89 | | | | | | |
| 90 | Widgets Mk2 - gross profit | | B13-(B77/2) | | IF(SUM(B90:M90)<>0,SUM(B90:M90),"") | |
| 91 | as % of sales | | B90/B13*100 | | M90/N13*100 | |
| 92 | | | | | | |
| 93 | | | B5 | | N5 | |

## Figure 8.22 (*BUDG01) Gross profit per product

| | A | | B | | C | | D | | E | | F | | G | | H | | I | | J | | K | | L | | M | | N | |
|---|---|---|---|---|---|---|---|---|---|---|---|---|---|---|---|---|---|---|---|---|---|---|---|---|---|---|---|---|
| 85 | | | | | | | | | | | | | | | | | | | | | | | | | | | | |
| 86 | BY PRODUCT | | | | | | | | | | | | | | | | | | | | | | | | | | | |
| 87 | Widgets Mk1 - gross profit | | 19100 | | 18850 | | 18650 | | 19100 | | 18850 | | 18750 | | 19100 | | 18850 | | 19000 | | 19100 | | 18850 | | 18750 | | 226950 | |
| 88 | as % of sales | | 35 | | 34 | | 34 | | 35 | | 35 | | 34 | | 35 | | 35 | | 35 | | 35 | | 35 | | 34 | | 34 | |
| 89 | | | | | | | | | | | | | | | | | | | | | | | | | | | | |
| 90 | Widgets Mk2 - gross profit | | 4100 | | 3850 | | 3650 | | 4100 | | 3850 | | 3750 | | 4100 | | 3850 | | 4000 | | 4100 | | 3850 | | 3750 | | 46950 | |
| 91 | as % of sales | | 10 | | 10 | | 10 | | 10 | | 10 | | 9 | | 10 | | 10 | | 10 | | 10 | | 10 | | 9 | | 10 | |
| 92 | | | | | | | | | | | | | | | | | | | | | | | | | | | | |
| 93 | | | Jan | | Feb | | Mar | | Apr | | May | | Jun | | Jul | | Aug | | Sep | | Oct | | Nov | | Dec | | Year | |

**Note:** because the addition of the profit calculation rows is a significant change, make another 'save' copy with the extension .SV4.

167

The gross profit per product from the new formulae are shown in Figure 8.22 (see page 167). Focus on the percentage of sales figures.

Widgets Mk1 are producing a gross profit of about 34 per cent on sales, and Widgets Mk2 only around 10 per cent.

This difference will create a number of fairly complex set of relationships when several changing factors take effect simultaneously. For now, only one change will be looked at.

In the first 'cause and effect' example the costs of both types of widget parts were reduced by 1.5 per cent month on month. We'll do exactly the same again, and look at the effect on the gross profitability of each. Just as before, in the budget forecast (★**BUDG01**) put **B29–(B29*.015)** in C29, and copy it down to C30 and across to column M.

Figure 8.23 (below) shows the gross profit percentage of sales for both widget types.

Note that, whereas the Mk1 profit has risen by about 6 per cent, the Mk2 has increased by about 8 per cent – for the same percentage reduction of parts cost.

168

**Figure 8.23 (★BUDG01 – Chart %GROSSPROD)**
**The same percentage parts cost reduction for Mk1 and Mk2**

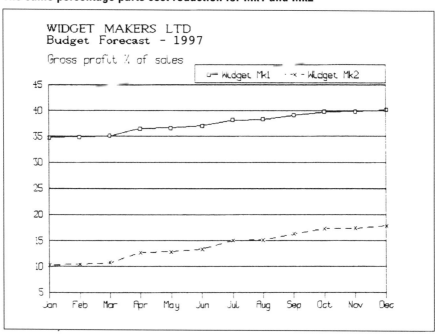

This *example is now finished* – restore the parts costs of Widgets Mk1 and Mk2 to their original values of £140 and £160 respectively.

## Summary

In this chapter:

- the purpose of the reiterative process has been explained;
- practical aspects of how to examine the effect of changes have been explored;
- a number of simple cause and effects that will be met in budget and cash flow forecasts were explored in detail;
- new rows were added to the budget forecast for calculating gross and net profit. A 'save' copy with the file extension .SV3 was then made of it;
- several examples of simple cause and effect were tried on the illustration computer models, including one that combined most of them in one forecast;

169

- additional formulae were created on the budget forecast for calculating the individual gross profit of each widget type. A 'save' copy with the file extension .SV4 was then made.

Start by including in the budget only those linked relationships that really can make a significant difference – it isn't worth trying to establish the arithmetic relationship between paper clips used per ream of paper – and follow up by separating spreadsheet models into departmental units only if it is really essential.

# 9
. . .

# Allocation, monitoring and reviewing

171

Budget allocation ■

Simple is best ■

Performance monitoring principles ■

Setting up monitoring for the Widget Makers Ltd forecast ■

Recording actual figures ■

Reviewing the forecast ■

# Budget allocation

■ ■ ■

The forecast has been built, checked, rechecked, revised and finally declared to be the best view of the year ahead that can be obtained. It is, therefore, ready for allocation and the status of an operational budget.

Operational budget status usually means that:

- fixed (capital, start up, constant direct and overhead) costs for each period must not be exceeded;
- intrinsic sales volumes for each period must be achieved;
- variable direct costs must not exceed the value determined by their arithmetic relationship with achieved sales volumes;
- a change can only be authorised by the budget's controller;

Of course, every company can, and will, determine precisely what a budget allocation means in its own organisation. As always in these matters, there is no right or wrong.

The budget may be split into departmental responsibilities, or maintained as a single entity. If split, there is still the option of either actually dividing the allocation up into departmental extracts, or keeping it as a single entity that every department receives, but in which their specific responsibilities are clearly identified.

The deciding factors in choosing are usually:

- the physical size and geographical split of the business;
- the size and complexity of individual departmental responsibilities;
- company policy.

If there is a 'right' and a 'wrong' of choice, it must be a goal of simplicity.

# Simple is best

■ ■ ■

There is no question whatever that in budget forecasting simple is best, but, unfortunately, the ease with which complex relationships and systems can be created with spreadsheets is also a potential Achilles' heel. I can make this point no more clearly than does Edward de Bono in the introduction to his book *The Mechanism of Mind*\*, in which he says:

---

\* Published by Jonathan Cape 1969, Simon and Schuster – New York 1969, Pelican Books 1971

Matters are often made more and more complex by the ability of man to play elaborate games that feed on themselves to create bewildering structures of immense intricacy, which obscure rather than reveal.

So keep things as simple as possible. Start by including in the budget only those linked relationships that really can make a significant difference – it isn't worth trying to establish the arithmetic relationship between paper clips used per ream of paper – and follow up by separating spreadsheet models into departmental units only if it really is essential.

If there is an ideal, it is to have a single budget that everyone who 'needs to know' has access to. Remember, however:

- if it has to be split for reasons of complexity, try to make it less complex;
- if it has to be split for reasons of size, try to make it smaller;
- if it has to be split for geographical reasons, don't forget about communications services like post, fax, telex, and electronic mail;
- if it has to be split to comply with company policy, check that the reasons for the company policy are well founded and not just habit.

173

And if it *still* needs to be split, make sure there are clear procedures in place with which the integrity of the whole will be maintained.

The importance of simplicity and maintaining an integrated whole becomes most apparent during monitoring and review – a good analogy is that of making a jigsaw puzzle. The creator of a puzzle can very easily make a large number of parts with very intricate shapes, just as it is very easy to build a very complex spreadsheet budget. But when the puzzle or spreadsheet are taken apart, they are then difficult to reassemble so that the whole picture can be clearly seen. The fewer the number of parts, the easier it is to consolidate back to a single entity.

For Widget Makers Ltd, a single forecast available to all of the senior managers was chosen in Chapter 5 (A Single or Departmental Budget?).

# Performance monitoring principles
■  ■  ■

I make no apology for once more repeating the only certainty of budget forecasts – they are wrong. Consequently, they must be checked, reviewed, and amended if necessary to ensure that they represent reality – or, rather, that they are as close to it as is practically and usefully achievable.

## Frequency of monitoring

In theory the frequency of checks and reviews depends to a large extent on the nature of the business, its financial dynamics, and the inherent probability of significant variations occurring in a given period. All very technical! In practice it is usually very easy indeed to at least decide the minimum interval between checks.

> The principle of monitoring is simply to compare what has actually been spent or earned, with what was forecast for each. This is why it is so important when creating the budget that expense and revenue headings are aligned with the source of actual figures, and that their periodicity is the same.

In fact, it is more than likely decided for you, unless you are responsible for bookkeeping policy, because that is where the actual data against which the forecast can be compared with, will probably come from.

When all is said and done, just about any business will benefit from, and not be overburdened by, a four-weekly or calendar-monthly monitoring cycle.

174

For Widget Makers Ltd a calendar-monthly period was chosen.

## The source of actual figures

The principle of monitoring is simply to compare what has actually been spent or earned, with what was forecast for each. This is why it is so important when creating the budget that expense and revenue headings are aligned with the source of actual figures, and that their periodicity is the same. If they are broken down in different ways, or do not use the same periods, comparison is at best very difficult, or at worst impossible.

The source of the actual performance figures depends upon the way in which each company operates, but they are usually obtained from either the ledgers – explained in Chapter 5 (Cost Headings) – of the company's accounts, or something similar that has been established for the purpose.

Widget Makers Ltd use the ledgers as the source of actual figures.

> **Note:** From here, references to the ledgers should be taken to include any other system that provides similar facilities, specifically – details of purchase and sales *invoices*, and purchase and sales *payments*.

## Invoices or payments?

In Chapter 1, under 'Cash Flow Forecasts' the offset in time that exists between when an expense is incurred, and cash is paid out for it, was explained, as was the similar offset between a sale and receipt of payment. And, of course, that these timing differences exist is the principal reason for having a cash flow forecast at all.

So, when collecting actual figures, should they be 'expense incurred' and 'sale made' – the *invoice* stage, or 'expense paid' and 'income received' – the *payment* stage, or both, or some combination of both?

Dealing with the straightforward circumstances first:

(a) If there is no cash flow forecast, then clearly there is little purpose in collecting cash payment and receipt figures. Actual data must be *invoice* details.

(b) Even if there *is* a cash flow forecast, but actual cash flow information is not available, then again there is no choice, actual data has to be *invoice* details.

(c) If invoice details are not available, then only *payment* details can be used.

*Circumstance (a)* presents no problem at all and will be fairly common in departments of larger companies.

*Circumstance (b)* is also fully workable, providing it is acceptable that the cash flow forecast can only ever be regarded as an indication of likely reality, but not as an accurate representation. Again, this is more likely to be a situation found in departments of larger companies, especially those that like their managers to be aware of the cash flow implications of the department's work.

*Circumstance (c)* will only be of practical forecasting use in a business that deals *exclusively* in cash, or only *always* pays invoices immediately they are received, and obtains immediate payment for its products. I can't think of any business at all that would meet these criteria, and therefore (c) as a likely circumstance will be ignored.

And then there is:

(d) With full access to the ledgers both *invoice* and *payment* details are available, and either or both may be used for monitoring purposes.

*Circumstance (d)* is the most likely to be found in medium to small companies, of which Widget Makers Ltd is an example.

The way in which the actual figures, whether *invoice* or *payment*, are recorded is dealt with later in this chapter.

## Comparing actual figures with the allocated budget

This section describes three fundamental ways in which actual figures can be compared with the allocated budget. The objective of them all is to retain a copy of the allocation, and to update the original copy with actual figures. The three methods are:

1 Paper budget copy.
2 Whole budget copy.
3 Key figure copy.

Before looking at these, there is another format to mention that may be familiar to you, and which you may think to try, especially if you have 'paper forecast' experience. It is also a format often used by high street banks in their advice packs to new business starters, *but it is not recommended for spreadsheet-based forecasts*. Figure 9.1 (below) illustrates the principle.

### Figure 9.1  Paper forecast collection of actual figures

|  | A | B | C | D | E | F | G |
|---|---|---|---|---|---|---|---|
| 1 | FILE : FIG9 | | | | | | |
| 2 | 28/10/1997 | | | | | | |
| 3 | | | Jan | | Feb | | Mar |
| 4 | | F'cst | Act | F'cst | Act | F'cst | Act |
| 5 | | | | | | | |
| 6 | Cost item 1 | 158 | 165 | 237 | 198 | 132 | |
| 7 | Cost item 2 | 53 | 48 | 80 | 73 | 44 | |
| 8 | Cost item 3 | 92 | 92 | 138 | 126 | 77 | |
| 9 | Cost item 4 | 354 | 344 | 531 | 564 | 295 | |
| 10 | Cost item 5 | 16 | 20 | 24 | 27 | 13 | |
| 11 | | | | | | | |
| 12 | Totals | 673 | 669 | 1010 | 988 | 561 | 0 |

**NOT RECOMMENDED FOR SPREADSHEET BASED FORECASTS**

The idea is to place the actual figures alongside their forecast values by dividing each month's column into two. Naturally, on a spreadsheet two separate columns must be used.

There are problems with using this format on a spreadsheet.

To start with it isn't very easy to distinguish between forecast and actual figures, especially if the whole year were shown. The format really needs vertical dividing lines between the months. In fact, on a paper version you would probably put a double dividing line between months, and a single line between forecast and actual.

Then there are the year totals for each row to consider. For instance, in row 8, the formulae for the *forecast* year total would be:

$$B8+D8+F8+H8+J8+L8+N8+P8+R8+T8+V8+X8$$

The SUM function can't be used because every alternate column must be skipped.

Similarly, the *actual* year total for the same row would be:

$$C8+E8+G8+I8+K8+M8+O8+Q8+S8+U8+W8+Y8$$

And any other function that depends on a contiguous sequence of cells couldn't be used either – *average* for instance.

Hopefully I have persuaded you not to use this format, now here are three viable methods.

## 1 Paper budget copy

A very easy way to keep a copy of the allocation – print a copy of each of the models on paper. That's it – job done!

## 2 Budget copy

This method looks complicated in its description, but in fact it can be done in just two or three minutes, certainly more quickly than I'll be able to write down how to do it.

The aim is to have three copies of each forecast on the same spreadsheet, one above the other. So each model's spreadsheet (Sales, Budget and Cash Flow) will look like it does in Figure 9.2 (below):

This is a way of creating the two additional copies, *but don't do it now*, read through for understanding, and return to it later if you need to.

**Figure 9.2 Three copies of the model**

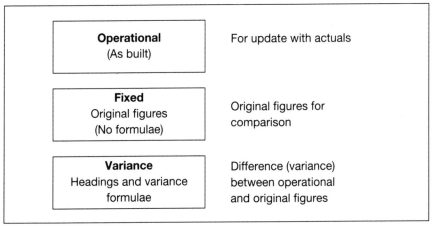

## Steps

1  Make a copy of the model below the 'operational', but *omit the formulae; copy the values only*. It is best to leave a reasonable number of rows empty between the bottom of the 'operational' and the top of the 'fixed' copy; perhaps ten or so, to lessen the risk of confusion between them.
2  Now, below the 'fixed' copy, again leaving some spare rows, make a copy of the row and column titles.

The *top version* is the operational one, and will be updated with actual figures where they are not picked up by the linking.

The *middle version* contains the fixed original figures, they will not be changed.

The *bottom version* – which at the moment consists of only the row and column headings – will be used to compare the actual figures in the 'operational' with the original figures in the 'fixed' version.

To enable this, note the cell addresses of the first data row for January in the operational and fixed versions, and in the corresponding cell of the variance version, enter a formulae that subtracts one from the other. Then copy the formulae down the rows and across the columns of the variance version. Figure 9.3 (below) illustrates the principle.

Initially the variance version will display all zeros, because the operational and fixed versions are still identical. As soon as anything is changed in the operational version, however, the difference between them and the fixed original figures will be displayed.

### Figure 9.3 Formulae to calculate variance

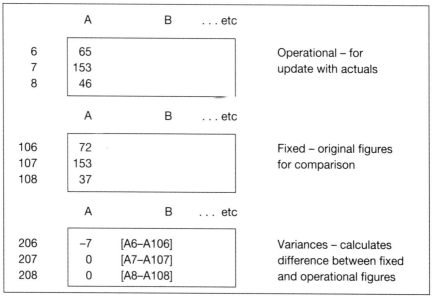

> **Tip:** *It is a good idea to set the variance version to display 'blank if zero', that way it is very much easier to read and to spot where variances occur.*

### 3 Key figure copy

This method uses exactly the same principle as 'Budget copy', except that instead of keeping a copy of all of the original figures, only those of major significance are kept for comparison with actuals. For instance, the total sales volume and value, each of the cost category subtotals, and the total cost.

Thus the steps for this method are very similar to 'Budget copy', except that only the key figure rows are reproduced for the fixed and variance versions.

## The pros and cons of each method

### 1 Paper copy

Has the advantage of being extremely easy to set up, but the disadvantage that manual methods must be used to calculate variances when actual figures are recorded on the spreadsheet.

### 2 Budget copy

Has the advantage of spreadsheet-calculated variances in full detail, but the disadvantage of being a little cumbersome and perhaps over detailed, especially if the spreadsheets are large.

### 3 Key figure copy

Has the advantage of spreadsheet-calculated variances, and being much less cumbersome than the full budget copy. Its only real disadvantage is that fully detailed variances are not available from it.

## Choosing a method

Whichever suits you best is the most honest answer, but remembering that 'simple is best', *my recommendation is to use a combination of 'paper copy' and 'key figure copy'*. This will provide automatic calculation of key variances, and if more detail is required, manual comparisons can be made between actual figures and the paper copy for any individual heading.

# Setting up monitoring for the Widget Makers Ltd forecast

■  ■  ■

The combination of 'paper copy' and 'key figure copy' will be used by Widget Makers Ltd, and so the first job is to make a paper copy of the allocated sales, budget and cash flow. Once that is done, the spreadsheet models can be set up. Again the detail of a written description can look a little daunting, but it really doesn't take more than about 15 minutes, with perhaps another 15 to 'tidy things up and make it look nice', and to test that everything works properly.

> ★ The monitoring copies of everything described here are already on the illustration disc versions ('P' suffix).

## Sales forecast

### Steps

1  Copy row 9 'Total Volume' to row 29, only the values (figures) are wanted, not the formulae.

2  Copy row 19 'Total Value' to row 31, again just the values.

3  Copy row 4 (month headings) to row 27.

4  Put the label 'ORIGINAL FIXED' in A26, and lines above and below this new block – in rows 25 and 32.

And that is the fixed original copy of the operational sales volumes and values. Because there are no formulae, they will not change, whatever happens elsewhere. Now for the variances block.

5  Copy rows 25:32 to row 34.

6  Replace the label in A35 with VARIANCES (Actual – Fixed Original)

7  These formulae subtract the figures in the middle (fixed) block from their corresponding figures in the top (operational) block:

In B38 enter **B9–B29**
In B40 enter **B19–B31**

and copy them both across to column N (Year Totals).

And that's it. Now, if any of the total volume or total value figures in the operational block are not the same as their corresponding figures in the fixed original block, their difference will be displayed in the variance block. Figure 9.4 (opposite) shows the two new blocks for the sales forecast.

**Figure 9.4 (*SALES01) Performance monitoring blocks – sales**

| | A | B | C | D | E | F | G | H | I | J | K | L | M | N |
|---|---|---|---|---|---|---|---|---|---|---|---|---|---|---|
| 25 | | | | | | | | | | | | | | |
| 26 | ORIGINAL FIXED | | | | | | | | | | | | | |
| 27 | *** SALES *** | Jan | Feb | Mar | Apr | May | Jun | Jul | Aug | Sep | Oct | Nov | Dec | Year Total |
| 28 | | | | | | | | | | | | | | |
| 29 | Total Volume | 300 | 300 | 300 | 300 | 300 | 300 | 300 | 300 | 300 | 300 | 300 | 300 | 3600 |
| 30 | | | | | | | | | | | | | | |
| 31 | Total Value £ | 95000 | 95000 | 95000 | 95000 | 95000 | 95000 | 95000 | 95000 | 95000 | 95000 | 95000 | 95000 | 1140000 |
| 32 | | | | | | | | | | | | | | |
| 33 | | | | | | | | | | | | | | |
| 34 | | | | | | | | | | | | | | |
| 35 | VARIANCES (Actual - Fixed Original) | | | | | | | | | | | | | Year |
| 36 | *** SALES *** | Jan | Feb | Mar | Apr | May | Jun | Jul | Aug | Sep | Oct | Nov | Dec | Total |
| 37 | | | | | | | | | | | | | | |
| 38 | Total Volume | 0 | 0 | 0 | 0 | 0 | 0 | 0 | 0 | 0 | 0 | 0 | 0 | 0 |
| 39 | | | | | | | | | | | | | | |
| 40 | Total Value £ | 0 | 0 | 0 | 0 | 0 | 0 | 0 | 0 | 0 | 0 | 0 | 0 | 0 |
| 41 | | | | | | | | | | | | | | |

## Budget forecast

### Steps

To make a copy of the key figure rows in the budget, either copy each row individually – in the same way as for the sales forecast, or, and this is the easiest way, copy all of the rows in one go and then delete those in the fixed original copy that are not wanted. Doing it the easy way:

1  Copy rows 5:69 to row 115, values only, the formulae are not wanted.

2  Add the label 'ORIGINAL FIXED' in A113, and put a line above the block, in row 112.

3  Delete all unwanted rows in the new block, leaving only these rows – see also Figure 9.5 (below):

   (a) Total sales volume and value.
   (b) Cost category headings and their subtotal row.
   (c) Total costs.
   (d) The dividing lines between categories.

**Figure 9.5 (★BUDG01)**
**Key figure headings for the budget forecast**

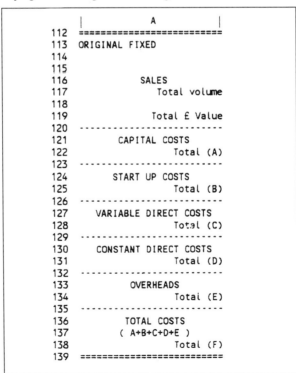

That completes the copy of the fixed original key figures of the budget forecast.

The variance block is going to have exactly the same key figure headings as the fixed block, and so that is the best place to copy it from.

**4** Copy rows 115:139 to row 148.

**5** Enter the label VARIANCES (Actual – Fixed Original) in A146, and put a line in row 145 to mark the top of the block.

**6** As in the sales forecast, enter formulae throughout the variance block, including the year totals, to subtract fixed block figures from their corresponding positions in the operational block. The formulae are shown in Figure 9.6 (below).

In the budget forecast another variance block is needed if there are variable direct costs, one that will compare the actual variable direct costs with the forecast value/item factor. For example, in our forecast, the 'Diesel fuel for deliveries' factor is £8 per widget sold. But, sales volumes will never be exactly as forecast, and it is also highly improbable that the cost of diesel fuel per widget will precisely match the forecast factor.

183

### Figure 9.6 (∗BUDG01)
### Variance formulae for the budget forecast

```
           A         ||   B   ||   C   ||   D   ||   E   ||   F   |
145  ==================================================================
146  VARIANCES (Actual - Fixed Original)
147
148                        Jan      Feb      Mar      Apr      May
149        SALES
150            Total volume B10-B117 C10-C117 D10-D117 E10-E117 F10-F117
151
152            Total £ Value B15-B119 C15-C119 D15-D119 E15-E119 F15-F119
153  -----------------------------------------------------------------
154        CAPITAL COSTS
155            Total (A) B21-B122 C21-C122 D21-D122 E21-E122 F21-F122
156  -----------------------------------------------------------------
157        START UP COSTS
158            Total (B) B26-B125 C26-C125 D26-D125 E26-E125 F26-F125
159  -----------------------------------------------------------------
160        VARIABLE DIRECT COSTS
161            Total (C) B42-B128 C42-C128 D42-D128 E42-E128 F42-F128
162  -----------------------------------------------------------------
163        CONSTANT DIRECT COSTS
164            Total (D) B51-B131 C51-C131 D51-D131 E51-E131 F51-F131
165  -----------------------------------------------------------------
166        OVERHEADS
167            Total (E) B64-B134 C64-C134 D64-D134 E64-E134 F64-F134
168  -----------------------------------------------------------------
169        TOTAL COSTS
170        ( A+B+C+D+E )
171            Total (F) B68-B138 C68-C138 D68-D138 E68-E138 F68-F138
172  ==================================================================
```

The aim, therefore, is to monitor any variable direct cost factors to check that they are about right. Several months' figures may be necessary to establish the trend. If any significant variance is noted, then of course the factors for the remaining months of the forecast can be adjusted accordingly.

The additional block is – 'Variable direct variances' – and can be put below the 'Variances' block. It needs to have the headings of each of the variable direct costs.

## Steps

**1** Copy A28:A32 to A180.

**2** Copy the month headings from row 5 to row 178.

**3** In A177 put the label 'VARIABLE DIRECT VARIANCES'.

**4** Put lines above and below the block in rows 176 and 185.

The formulae are required to subtract the forecast cost per item from the actual cost per item. Remember that 'Diesel fuel' and 'Wages (Temporary staff)' operate on the total widget volumes.

**5** Enter these formulae (see also Figure 9.7 below), and copy to column M (December):

| Row | Title | Formulae |
| --- | --- | --- |
| 181 | Parts for Widgets Mk1 | (B37/B7)–B29 |
| 182 | Parts for Widgets Mk2 | (B38/B8)–B30 |
| 183 | Diesel fuel (Deliveries) | (B39/B10)–B31 |
| 184 | Wages (Temporary staff) | (B40/B10)–B32 |

**6** Because the numbers displayed may be less than one, format the block to two decimal places.

### Figure 9.7 (★BUDG01)
### Row headings and formulae for variable direct variances

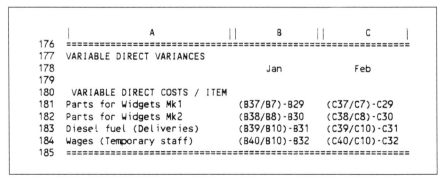

Now, if any of the actual factors are different to the forecast values, and in practice they almost certainly will be, the difference will be displayed in this block.

Figure 9.7 shows the row headings and formulae.

## Cash flow forecast

### Steps

All of the necessary key figure information for the cash flow forecast is contained within its 'Cash Flow and Bank' section.

1   Copy rows 56:65 to row 81, values only, the formulae are not wanted.
2   Add the label 'ORIGINAL FIXED' in A82.

That completes the copy of the fixed original block for the cash flow forecast.

The variance block is going to have exactly the same key figure headings as the fixed block.

3   Copy rows 81:92 to row 96.
4   Enter the label VARIANCES (Actual – Fixed Original) in A97.
5   As before, enter formulae throughout the variances block, including the year totals, to subtract fixed block figures from their corresponding positions in the operational block. The formulae are shown in Figure 9.8 (see page 186).

And that completes the monitoring blocks for the cash flow forecast.

Figure 9.8 shows the fixed original and variances block row headings, and the variance formulae.

The spreadsheets are now ready to receive actual performance figures.

> **Note:** Significant changes have been made. Make 'save' copies of all of the spreadsheets with the file extension .SV5

## Recording actual figures
■ ■ ■

Earlier on, the question of whether to record actual *invoices or payments* was considered, and found to be partly dependent on which were available. For Widget Makers Ltd we will assume that both are available from the ledgers, but the methods described will be equally applicable to any circumstance.

**Figure 9.8 (\*CASH01) The monitoring blocks and formulae for the cash flow**

|  | A | B | C | D | E | F | G |
|---|---|---|---|---|---|---|---|
| 81 | | Jan | Feb | Mar | Apr | May | Jun |
| 82 | ORIGINAL FIXED | | | | | | |
| 83 | | | | | | | |
| 84 | CASH FLOW AND BANK | | | | | | |
| 85 | | | | | | | |
| 86 | Net cash flow | 4625 | 4000 | -46075 | -5375 | -5700 | 1925 |
| 87 | | | | | | | |
| 88 | Balance B/F | 35000 | 39625 | 43625 | -2450 | -7825 | -13525 |
| 89 | Cash In | 95000 | 95000 | 95000 | 95000 | 95000 | 95000 |
| 90 | Cash Out | 90375 | 91000 | 141075 | 100375 | 100700 | 93075 |
| 91 | Balance C/F | 39625 | 43625 | -2450 | -7825 | -13525 | -11600 |
| 92 | | | | | | | |
| 93 | | | | | | | |
| 94 | | | | | | | |
| 95 | | | | | | | |
| 96 | | | | | | | |
| 97 | VARIANCES (Actual - Fixed Original) | | | | | | |
| 98 | | | | | | | |
| 99 | CASH FLOW AND BANK | Jan | Feb | Mar | Apr | May | Jun |
| 100 | | | | | | | |
| 101 | Net cash flow | B59-B86 | C59-C86 | D59-D86 | E59-E86 | F59-F86 | G59-G86 |
| 102 | | | | | | | |
| 103 | Balance B/F | B61-B88 | C61-C88 | D61-D88 | E61-E88 | F61-F88 | G61-G88 |
| 104 | Cash In | B62-B89 | C62-C89 | D62-D89 | E62-E89 | F62-F89 | G62-G89 |
| 105 | Cash Out | B63-B90 | C63-C90 | D63-D90 | E63-E90 | F63-F90 | G63-G90 |
| 106 | Balance C/F | B64-B91 | C64-C91 | D64-D91 | E64-E91 | F64-F91 | G64-G91 |
| 107 | | | | | | | |

**Table 9.1 Widget Makers Ltd – January period end actual figures**

| | |
|---|---|
| **SALES** | |
| Widget Mk1 sales volumes | 206 |
| Widget Mk2 sales volumes | 92 |
| Widget Mk1 sales value | 56650 |
| Widget Mk2 sales value | 36800 |
| | |
| **EXPENSES** | |
| | |
| **Capital costs** | |
| Factory machinery | – |
| Office machinery | – |
| | |
| **Start up costs** | |
| Design of Widget Mk3 | – |
| | |
| **Variable direct costs** | |
| Parts for Widgets Mk1 | 28840 |
| Parts for Widgets Mk2 | 14720 |
| Diesel fuel (Deliveries) | 2450 |
| Wages (Temporary staff) | 3900 |
| | |
| **Constant direct costs** | |
| Electricity | – |
| Gas | – |
| Machine maintenance (Factory) | 600 |
| Salaries (Widget production) | 19750 |
| Vehicle maintenance (Delivery) | 3500 |
| | |
| **Overheads** | |
| Building maintenance | 150 |
| Machine maintenance (Office) | 100 |
| Petrol (Manager's cars) | 550 |
| Postage | 25 |
| Rates | 200 |
| Salaries (Management) | 17000 |
| Stationery | 210 |
| Telephone | – |
| Vehicle maintenance (Managers) | – |

Rather than looking at the theory, it is probably best to run through the collection and recording of the one month's actual figures from beginning to end. We may as well start with January.

Early in February the following actual performance figures for January become available. All revenue and expense items are *invoice* figures, not cash payments or receipts. *And don't forget, the actual figures must be exclusive of VAT.*

To update the forecast then, it is just a matter of entering these figures in place of the forecast values for January.

**Important:** Sometimes forecast figures occur in more than one place, for instance 'Sales Volume' and 'Sales Value' are in the sales forecast *and* in the budget forecast. The rule is to overwrite the forecast at the lowest point in the system's hierarchy, and allow the links to update any dependents. In the case of the sales figures, this is the sales forecast model SALES01. The linkages will automatically update the dependent spreadsheet BUDG01.

★ Note for users of the illustration disc. The 'actual' figures are not written into your models.

## Steps

1   Enter the actual sales volume and value figures in SALES01. Note that the actual sales values are identical to the forecast once the actual volumes are in. This is because the widgets were sold at the expected price. However, it is a good discipline to nevertheless overwrite the formulae that is calculating the value with the actual figure, because it can then be clearly seen at a later date that the actual fig ures for the month *were* considered.

2   Enter the actual expenses in BUDG01.

Again, where the actual is the same as a calculated forecast figure, overwrite the formulae with the actual figure. And where there is no actual figure where one was forecast, enter a zero.

And that's it, all of the month's actual figures in, and it only took about five minutes.

The next job is to *look* at the forecast and see what it tells us.

# Reviewing the forecast
■ ■ ■

The word *look* in the last sentence is highlighted for a very good reason, it is stressing the importance of studying the results of actual data entry, of looking for the tell-tale signs that things are progressing satisfactorily, or going wrong. It's unlikely that this will be a problem when you first start to use the forecast, its new, and you will probably spend hours exploring the first month or two of results.

But here is the danger. It usually takes a few months of actual data entry before steady trends are established, or before the factors and assumptions start to reveal their inherent errors. Before that point is reached, and the novelty of having all this financial control information available starts to wear off – especially because 'nothing much seems to be happening' – the monthly review may have become so routine that you only give the results a cursory glance before consigning them to a file.

Worse – much, much worse. You may even have delegated monthly data entry to someone who has no responsibility for, or expertise in, what the forecasts are showing. Disaster!

> It usually takes a few months of actual data entry before steady trends are established, or before the factors and assumptions start to reveal their inherent errors.

If you really, absolutely, categorically, positively, 'no other way' must delegate the monthly data entry (it only takes a few minutes for goodness sake) to someone else, then it is even more important that you: **look, really look, each month, at the forecasts as soon as the latest figures have been entered.**

There are no special rules for what to look at, every company and every forecast is different. But you *will* see when things are going wrong, so long as you look carefully. And there is no better way of keeping in tune with the figures, line by line, than by entering the monthly figures yourself. Don't regard it as simply one of those 'easy' jobs that can be given to the office junior, these are the life blood details of the company, and they deserve your personal attention and expertise in their analysis.

OK – enough of the preaching, let's get back to *looking* (sorry – slip of the keyboard, I meant *LOOKING* !) at what has happened to the Widget Makers Ltd forecast now that the first month's figures are in – see Figure 9.9 (page 191).

All of the relevant information is in the budget forecast, here is the operational section of the budget. The figures that are different to the original (Figure 7.2) are in bold characters.

Now, the fact that many of the figures are different is no surprise at all, the majority will vary from the forecast every month. What's important is by *how much* they are different, and of course that is why the calculation of variance blocks have been included. Not only do they show that a variance exists, but also the magnitude of it.

## Budget variances

Figure 9.10 (see page 192) shows the budget's variance and variable direct variance blocks.

My spreadsheet is set up to show negative values in parenthesese, they stand out more than a minus sign.

Note that in all cases, a *negative variance* means that the actual is *less* than the original budget.

Looking at each of the key figure variances:

## Total sales volume

Under budget by 2 in 300, no cause for concern here. Though we do note from the detail in Figure 9.9 that Widgets Mk2 volumes were eight under budget, that's a 4 per cent forecast error. Look at this carefully next month.

## Total sales value

Under budget by £1,550 – exactly as expected for the sales volumes achieved.

## Capital

No expenditure as forecast.

## Start up

No expenditure as forecast.

## Variable direct costs

Under budget by £990. A lower figure would be expected in view of the below forecast volumes, but is all of it due to volume? It could be worked out, but there is no need, the variable direct variances will tell us when we look at them.

## Constant direct costs

Over budget by £2,950 – that's quite a lot, and we can't see from the key figure variances what has caused it. But looking back to the original budget (Figure 7.2) and comparing the figures for constant directs in January, we see that whilst Salaries (Widget production) are under budget by £250, Vehicle maintenance (Delivery) is over budget by £3,200. Speaking to the transport manager reveals that one of the vans needed a new engine.

## Figure 9.9 (★BUDG01)
## The budget with January's actual figures entered

```
     |        A          || B  || C  || D  || E  || F  |
  1   | FILE : BUDG01P.xls         W I D G E T   M A K E R S   L T D
  2   |   30/10/1996                Budget Forecast - 1997
  3   |   12:01pm
  4   |
  5   |                        Jan      Feb     Mar     Apr     May
  6   |         SALES
  7   | Volume - Widgets Mk1    206      200     200     200     200
  8   | Volume - Widgets Mk2     92      100     100     100     100
  9   | (Spare)
 10   |         Total volume    298      300     300     300     300
 11   |
 12   | Value - Widgets Mk1    56650    55000   55000   55000   55000
 13   | Value - Widgets Mk2    36800    40000   40000   40000   40000
 14   | (Spare)
 15   |        Total £ Value   93450    95000   95000   95000   95000
 16   | --------------------------------------------------------------
 17   |      CAPITAL COSTS
 18   | Factory machinery                        50000
 19   | Office machinery                                          5000
 20   | (Spare)
 21   |           Total (A)       0        0    50000       0     5000
 22   | --------------------------------------------------------------
 23   |      START UP COSTS
 24   | Design of Widget Mk3                            10000     2000
 25   | (Spare)
 26   |           Total (B)       0        0        0   10000     2000
 27   | --------------------------------------------------------------
 28   | VARIABLE DIRECT COSTS / ITEM
 29   | Parts for Widgets Mk1    140      140     140     140     140
 30   | Parts for Widgets Mk2    160      160     160     160     160
 31   | Diesel fuel (Deliveries)   8        8       8       8       8
 32   | Wages (Temporary staff)   15       15      15      15      15
 33   | (Spare)
 34   |
 35   |     VARIABLE DIRECT COSTS
 36   |       (Vol x Cost / Item)
 37   | Parts for Widgets Mk1   28840    28000   28000   28000   28000
 38   | Parts for Widgets Mk2   14720    16000   16000   16000   16000
 39   | Diesel fuel (Deliveries) 2450     2400    2400    2400    2400
 40   | Wages (Temporary staff)  3900     4500    4500    4500    4500
 41   | (Spare)
 42   |           Total (C)    49910    50900   50900   50900   50900
 43   | --------------------------------------------------------------
 44   |    CONSTANT DIRECT COSTS
 45   | Electricity                      500                      500
 46   | Gas                                      900
 47   | Machine maintenance (Factory)  600  600     600     600     600
 48   | Salaries (Widget production) 19750 20000  20000   20000   20000
 49   | Vehicle maintenance (Delivery) 3500 300     300     300     300
 50   | (Spare)
 51   |           Total (D)    23850    21400   21800   20900   21400
 52   | --------------------------------------------------------------
 53   |        OVERHEADS
 54   | Building maintenance     150      400     400     400    2900
 55   | Machine maintenance (Office) 100  100     100     100     100
 56   | Petrol (Manager's cars)  550      600     600     600     600
 57   | Postage                   25       90      90      90      90
 58   | Rates                    200                      200     200
 59   | Salaries (Management)   17000    17000   17000   17000   17000
 60   | Stationery               210       85      85      85      85
 61   | Telephone                        325                     325
 62   | Vehicle maintenance (Managers)  0  100     100     100     100
 63   | (Spare)
 64   |           Total (E)    18235    18700   18375   18575   21400
 65   | --------------------------------------------------------------
 66   |      TOTAL COSTS
 67   |     ( A+B+C+D+E )
 68   |           Total (F)    91995    91000  141075  100375  100700
 69   | ==============================================================
```

### Figure 9.10 (∗BUDG01)
### The budget's variance blocks reflecting January actual data

```
145  ========================================================================
146  VARIANCES (Actual - Fixed Original)
147
148                              Jan      Feb      Mar      Apr      May
149          SALES
150              Total volume (     2)
151
152              Total £ Value (  1550)
153  ------------------------------------------------------------------------
154          CAPITAL COSTS
155                  Total (A)
156  ------------------------------------------------------------------------
157          START UP COSTS
158                  Total (B)
159  ------------------------------------------------------------------------
160          VARIABLE DIRECT COSTS
161                  Total (C) (   990)
162  ------------------------------------------------------------------------
163          CONSTANT DIRECT COSTS
164                  Total (D)   2950
165  ------------------------------------------------------------------------
166              OVERHEADS
167                  Total (E) (   340)
168  ------------------------------------------------------------------------
169              TOTAL COSTS
170          ( A+B+C+D+E )
171                  Total (F)   1620
172  ========================================================================
173
174
175
176  ========================================================================
177  VARIABLE DIRECT VARIANCES
178                              Jan      Feb      Mar      Apr      May
179
180  VARIABLE DIRECT COSTS / ITEM
181  Parts for Widgets Mk1
182  Parts for Widgets Mk2
183  Diesel fuel (Deliveries)      .22
184  Wages (Temporary staff)    (1.91)
185  ■_ __==========================================================================
```

192

## Overheads

Under budget by £340, not really a big enough variance to get concerned about, though out of interest a quick glance down the paper original (Figure 7.2) shows that the variances were:

| | |
|---|---:|
| Building maintenance | (250) |
| Petrol (Managers' cars) | (50) |
| Postage | (65) |
| Stationery | 125 |
| Vehicle maintenance (Mgrs) | (100) |

## Total costs

The net effect of all of the cost variances is £1,620 over budget.

Now to look at those variable direct variances.

## Parts for Widgets Mk1 and Mk2

No variance, the parts costs were exactly as expected.

## Diesel fuel (Deliveries)

The forecast uses a factor of £8 per widget, and the variance is showing that the cost was actually 22p more than that. It's quite possible that over the next few months the cumulative variance will move nearer to £8, if it doesn't, then a revised factor should be entered for the remainder of the year. Nothing to worry about yet though.

## Wages (Temporary staff)

The forecast uses a factor of £15 per widget, the variance for January was £1.91 less. Again, two or three more months' figures are probably required to get a settled trend and average. Leave the forecast factor as it is for now, but keep an eye on it.

Right, that's all of the revenue and expense variances looked at, but what about profitability?

## Profitability

One month of actual data isn't really sufficient to get a meaningful picture, but we'll take a look anyway. Remember there was a new engine for a delivery vehicle that is part of constant direct costs, so we would expect both gross and net profit to have been affected by it. Figure 9.11 (see page 194) shows the profit section of the budget forecast.

Yes, about 3 per cent off overall profits compared to the original (Figure 8.3), but look at the 'By Product' figures. Widgets Mk1 are still at 35 per cent of sales, but Widgets Mk2 have hit the deck! In fact they show a small gross loss of £80.

**Figure 9.11 (∗BUDG01)**
**Profit calculations for January**

| | A | B | C | D | E | F |
|---|---|---|---|---|---|---|
| 72 | | | | | | |
| 73 | PROFITABILITY | Jan | Feb | Mar | Apr | May |
| 74 | (Excluding capital and start up) | | | | | |
| 75 | | | | | | |
| 76 | Revenue from sales | 93450 | 95000 | 95000 | 95000 | 95000 |
| 77 | Direct costs | 73760 | 72300 | 72700 | 71800 | 72300 |
| 78 | Gross profit | 19690 | 22700 | 22300 | 23200 | 22700 |
| 79 | as % of sales | 21 | 24 | 23 | 24 | 24 |
| 80 | | | | | | |
| 81 | Overhead costs | 18235 | 18700 | 18375 | 18575 | 21400 |
| 82 | Total costs | 91995 | 91000 | 91075 | 90375 | 93700 |
| 83 | Net profit | 1455 | 4000 | 3925 | 4625 | 1300 |
| 84 | as % of sales | 2 | 4 | 4 | 5 | 1 |
| 85 | | | | | | |
| 86 | BY PRODUCT | | | | | |
| 87 | Widgets Mk1 - gross profit | 19770 | 18850 | 18650 | 19100 | 18850 |
| 88 | as % of sales | 35 | 34 | 34 | 35 | 34 |
| 89 | | | | | | |
| 90 | Widgets Mk2 - gross profit | -80 | 3850 | 3650 | 4100 | 3850 |
| 91 | as % of sales | 0 | 10 | 9 | 10 | 10 |
| 92 | | | | | | |
| 93 | | Jan | Feb | Mar | Apr | May |

The reason for this is obvious from inspection of the models. The constant direct costs (remember the new van engine) are shared equally between Mk1s and Mk2s, but the gross profit of sales for the Mk2 was only about 10 per cent, compared with the Mk1's 35 per cent (Figure 8.22). And what's more, the sales in January for the Mk2s were down eight, whilst the Mk1s were up six.

## Cash flow

Now for a look at the impact of the January figures on cash flow. Remember that we have only entered *invoice* figures, not payments nor receipts, and so the cash flow forecast will *not necessarily be reflecting actual cash flow*, to obtain that, the *payment* figures for January must be obtained and entered. More of that later, for now we'll look at the effect so far. Figure 9.12 shows the variance section of the cash flow forecast after the entry of actual January data in the sales and budget forecasts.

Remember – this is the difference between the original forecast, and the impact of the January invoice details in the sales and budget forecasts.

## Figure 9.12 (★CASH01)
## The variance section of the cash flow forecast

```
96   =============================================================
97   VARIANCES (Actual - Fixed Original)
98
99           CASH FLOW AND BANK          Jan      Feb      Mar      Apr      May
100  --------------------------------------------------------------------
101  Net cash flow                  (  3610) ( 1600)
102  --------------------------------------------------------------------
103  Balance B/F                             (  3610) (  5210) (  5210) (  5210)
104  Cash In                        (  1550) (  1550)
105  Cash Out                          2060       50
106  Balance C/F                    (  3610) (  5210) (  5210) (  5210) (  5210)
107  =============================================================
```

## Net cash flow

A total of £3,610 less net cash has flown through the business. Net cash flow is the sum of *cash in* and *cash out*.

## Balance B/F

As this is the first month, there will be no change to the balance brought forward.

## Cash in

£1,550 less cash came into the business than forecast.

## Cash out

£2,060 more cash went out of the business than forecast.

## Balance C/F

The balance carried forward is different to the forecast by the same amount as the Net Cash Flow + Balance B/F variances.

And there is really little else to be said about the cash flow. As long as it remains wholly dependent upon the budget forecast, then the impact on it will be driven entirely by the offset of the links between them. But remember that it is *not* a literal representation of cash flow, only notional based on the offsets.

If a true picture of cash flow is needed, then the actual *payment* figures (meaning cash payments and receipts) must be entered in the cash flow operational block, overwriting the link formulae to the budget. **Don't forget, the actual figures must be exclusive of VAT**.

The method is exactly the same as for the budget, and there is no need to repeat it. However, if actual payment and receipt figures are going to be put in, then another facility becomes available from the system – the calculation of accruals and prepayments.

## Accruals

An *expense accrual* is the amount of money owed, but not yet paid, for goods or services already received.

A *sales accrual* is the amount of money owed, but not yet received, for goods or services already supplied to a customer.

Providing that actual cash flow details have been entered, the forecasting and monitoring system contains all of the information required to calculate how accruals stand, or will stand, in any period.

*To calculate expense accruals* to any given period:

**(Total budget forecast costs – (Total cash flow forecast payments
to the period)** **to the period)**

their difference is what has yet to be paid.

Expense accrual example:

|  | Jan | Feb | Mar | Apr | £ Total |
|---|---|---|---|---|---|
| Budget cost | 500 | 200 | 300 | 400 | **1400** |
| Cash paid | 300 | 100 | 200 | 500 | **1100** |

Expense accruals at April = £1,400 – £1,100 = £300

*To calculate sales accruals* to any given period:

**(Total budget forecast sales – (Total cash flow forecast receipts
to the period)** **to the period)**

their difference is what has yet to be received:

Sales accrual example:

|  | Jan | Feb | Mar | Apr | £ Total |
|---|---|---|---|---|---|
| Budget sales | 2000 | 3000 | 2500 | 3000 | **10500** |
| Cash received | 1500 | 2500 | 3000 | 2000 | **9000** |

Sales accruals at April = £10,500 – £9,000 = £1,500

Finally, the current assets of the company can be calculated for the period end simply by:

**Balance C/F + Sales accruals – Expense accruals**

It doesn't matter if either expense or sales accruals are minus values, the sum still works out.

A minus value expense accrual is sometimes called a purchase prepayment, it means that cash has been paid before goods or services have been received.

A minus value sales accrual is sometimes called a sales prepayment, it means that cash has been received in advance of supplying goods or services.

## Summary

In this chapter:

- the budget has been allocated using the principle of a single budget available to everyone who needs to know, and the objective of simplicity;

- three viable methods of retaining a copy of the original budget were discussed, and a combination of 'paper' and 'key figure copy' was chosen for Widget Makers Ltd;

- the necessary modifications to the sales, budget and cash flow forecasts were made, and 'save' copies taken with a .SV5 file extension;

- actual 'invoice' figures for January were entered in the sales and budget forecasts, and the results examined;

- the impact of the January actual figures on the cash flow were discussed, and it was shown that entry of actual 'payment' figures into the cash flow is identical, in principle, to that for the budget;

- the concept of accruals was explored, and it was seen that budget and cash flow forecasts together provide all information necessary for their calculation.

The most important thing to remember in 'What-if'ing' is that it will only generate realistic predictions if all of the significant factors that impact on it are built into the model.

# 10
# . . .
# Further analysis

The impact of change on cash flow ■  199

The effect of rapid growth on cash flow ■

What-if analysis ■

# The impact of change on cash flow
■ ■ ■

The budget forecast set up for Widget Makers Ltd has a flat sales profile, the same volume of sales for each month of the year. This is not of course realistic, most businesses experience volume changes of some sort – they may just be fluctuations above and below a steady annual average, increases through growth, decreases through falling business, or perhaps seasonal variations. Or, during the forecast's span, a combination of all of them.

When all of these factors are operating together the resulting effect on cash flow is quite complex, and certainly difficult to visualise. The combined effects could of course be described in detail, but you wouldn't thank me for it, it's far better just to produce a graph that shows the relevant figures. However, the basic principles operating to create the effects is very simple indeed, and very well worthwhile looking at.

The original Widget Makers Ltd forecast can be used, but only the figures directly affected need be considered, these are:

- sales volume (total);
- cash in (from sales);
- cash out (for widget parts).

> **Note:** I'll use the terms 'Cash In' and 'Cash Out' in the explanation, but remember that Cash Out means for widget parts only in this section.

By looking initially at just these figures, the explanation of the principles won't be confused by the overlaid effects of everything else in the budget forecast.

This is how the timing offsets of Cash In and Cash Out are related to sales for Widget Makers Ltd:

|  | May | June | July |
|---|---|---|---|
| Cash Out | XX |  |  |
| Sales |  | XX |  |
| Cash In |  |  | XX |

Cash is paid out for widget parts one month before the sale is shown in the forecast, and cash is received in from the sales one month after.

I have set up a graph in the cash flow forecast that shows just the relevant figures (it takes sales volumes from the sales forecast using file

links). There are no values on the Y axis because they are not important, it is the shape of each line with respect to the others that we will
be looking at.

## Flat sales profile

Figure 10.1 (below) shows how it looks for the original flat sales volumes.
Note that 'Minimum balance' and 'Annual net cash flow' are still shown,
and their values are of course the same as when the budget was first com-
piled in Figure 7.5.

**Figure 10.1 (∗CASH01 – Chart 2)**
**Widget Makers Ltd – flat sales profile**

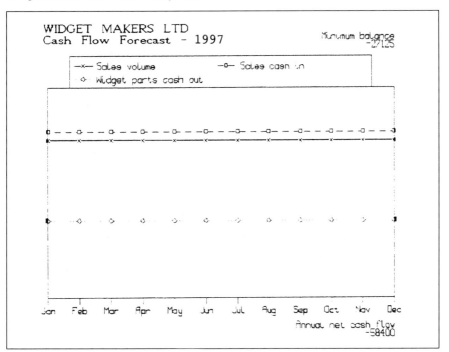

## Sales volume peaks

To illustrate the effect of volume changes, we'll first of all put an increase
in just one month, from 200 to 1000 Widgets Mk1 in June. The increase
of 800 Widgets Mk1 is perhaps unrealistically large, but it helps to highlight the effect. Figure 10.2 (overleaf) shows what happens, and it can be
clearly seen that the *cash out* peak is occurring one month before the
additional sales, and the *cash in* for them one month later.

**Figure 10.2 ★CASH01 – Chart 2)**
**Additional 800 Widgets Mk1 in June**

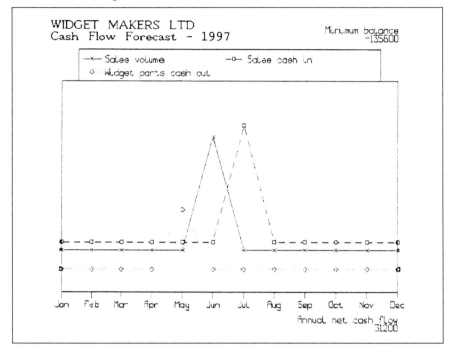

202

Also, look at the Annual net cash flow, it is now a healthy positive number as a result of the large June sales. But the minimum balance has
dropped through the floor from –£27127 in Figure 7.5 to –£135,600!

A thousand sales of Mk1 widgets in June, better annual net cash flow
– how can the minimum bank balance have fallen to that level? It's
because the parts for the additional 800 Widgets Mk1 in June had to be
paid for in May. We'll look more closely at this effect a little later.

Some business types may experience large 'one off' peaks of sales, others will have more gradual changes.

## Smooth sales growth

Figure 10.3 shows the effect of smooth sales volume growth of Widgets
Mk1 from January to June, and reversion to the original monthly
volumes from July onwards.

The growth from January to June has been deliberately set so that the
total widgets sold in the year is virtually the same as in the previous
single increase example.

**Figure 10.3 (∗CASH01 – Chart 2)**
**Smooth growth until June**

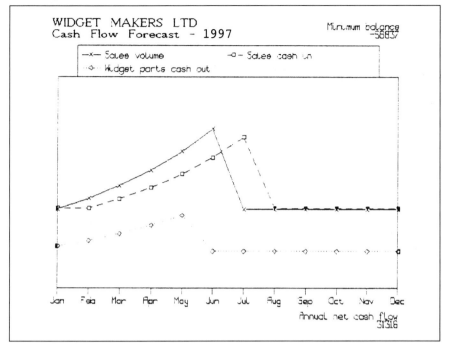

In this case, Annual net cash flow is very similar to the single increase example, but the minimum balance has improved very considerably. Yet the total sales, and hence *profit, in both cases is exactly the same*.

Thus, different profiles of the same levels of sales have markedly different effects on cash flow.

## The overall effect of sales volume changes

Now, having examined the principles, let's look again at the whole picture with each version of the additional 800 sales.

Figure 10.4 (overleaf) shows the single increase, and Figure 10.5 (on page 205) the smooth growth from January until June (these graphs have a different scale to Figure 7.5).

If this were a real bank account, the year end balance for the single increase version would be lower than for the smooth increase version, because of higher overdraft charges. Clearly it would be a good idea to add a bank overdraft interest calculation to the cash flow forecast in a case like this.

**Figure 10.4 (★CASH01 – Chart 1)**
**Single peak increase of 800 widgets**

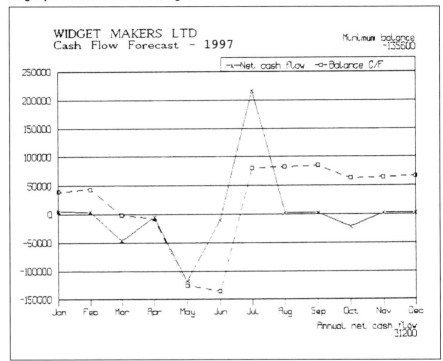

204

## Earlier and later sales receipts

In Chapter 8 (Further Examples of Cause and Effect) the impact of overhead payment timing changes on cash flow were illustrated. The effect of timing changes on sales volume related items would be very similar to those on overheads for a flat sales profile, but conspicuously different when applied to a growth profile.

> **Earlier cash payments or later sales receipts will very significantly worsen cash flow, and conversely, later cash payments or earlier sales receipts will significantly improve it.**

Earlier cash payments or later sales receipts will very significantly worsen cash flow, and conversely, later cash payments or earlier sales receipts will significantly improve it.

**Figure 10.5 (★CASH01 – Chart 1)**
**Smooth growth increase of 800 widgets**

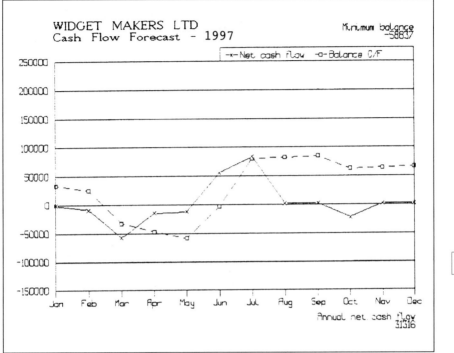

WIDGET MAKERS LTD
Cash Flow Forecast - 1997

Minimum balance −58837

-×- Net cash flow  -□- Balance C/F

Annual net cash flow 31316

We'll use just earlier and later sales receipts on the same January to June growth in the previous example to illustrate the principle.

# Earlier

Figure 10.6 (see page 206) shows the effect of one month earlier sales receipts. Whilst Annual net cash flow is unaffected because the growth is only in the first part of the year, the minimum balance has improved by about £50,000 to just −£7,918.

Figure 10.7 (see page 206) shows the effect of one month later sales receipts. Again, Annual net cash flow is not affected (another dummy figure had to be put into February Cash In), the minimum balance has worsened by £41,000 to −£99,592. Again this would have very severe implications for interest charges in a bank account.

**Figure 10.6 (★CASH01 – Chart 1)**
**One month earlier sales receipts**

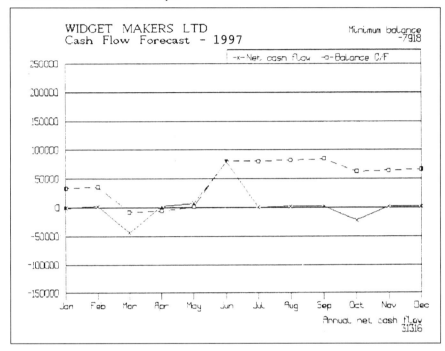

**Figure 10.7 (★CASH01 – Chart 1)**
**One month later sales receipts**

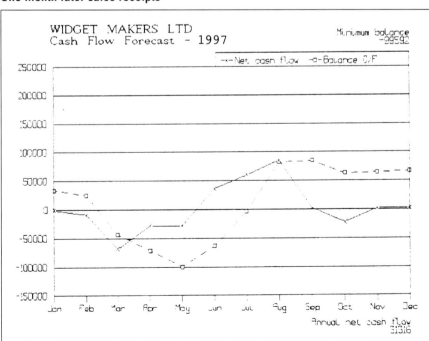

# The effect of rapid growth on cash flow
■ ■ ■

Finally, in this section, we'll have a look at the effect of growth to the point where cash flow goes into 'reverse', and the bank balance gets worse month by month, although the business is in fact still profitable.

This effect is driven by a volume growth steep enough that the cash received for earlier sales is insufficient to cover the direct costs – that must be paid for in advance, for the greater quantity of sales orders ahead – after constant and overhead expenses have been paid.

The level of growth required to cause reverse cash flow is a combined function of, and the relationships between:

■ cost of direct variables;

■ timing of payment for direct variable costs;

■ net profit;

■ overheads;

■ timing of sales receipts.

Generally, the conditions susceptible to reverse cash flow are low net profit margins, variable direct costs a high proportion of total direct costs, overheads small compared to total costs, and high debtor days (the time taken for sales invoices to be paid).

In Figure 10.8 (see page 208), rather than meddle with Widget Makers' fairly comfortable circumstances, which aren't especially susceptible to reverse cash flow, I have introduced a rather impracticably high sales growth to illustrate the effect. This also shows that even a comfortable business cannot afford to be complacent if faced with an opportunity for rapid growth.

The growth is 50 per cent month on month, for widgets Mk1 and Mk2, from January through to September, after which the volumes are restored to their starting values of 300 widgets total per month. Cutting growth off in September illustrates the extraordinary effect as the tidal wave of cash owed to the business floods in.

## Tell the bank what's happening

A principal reason for needing to understand this effect is so that a coherent rationale for borrowing requirements, in this case, of more than three quarters of a million pounds, (see the minimum balance) can be presented to the provider of funds. You must show them that although your borrowing requirements are increasing rapidly, the reason is profitable growth. A bank manager for instance who is not informed about what is

**Figure 10.8 (★CASH01 – Chart 1)**
**Fifty per cent sales growth from January to September**

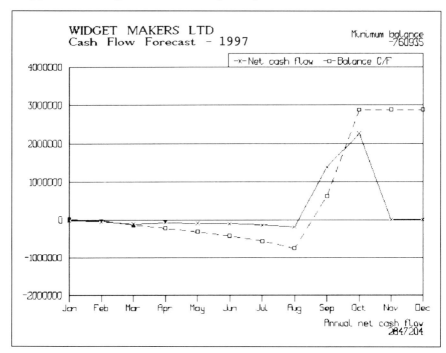

208

happening, is just as likely to regard a rising overdraft as indicative of the business' poor profitability, assuming they look at the statements and see the sales receipts on it, or as a declining business if they don't.

The moral – make sure your provider of cash funding understands what is happening in the business.

# 'What-if' analysis

■ ■ ■

Very often a forecast will be created solely for the purpose of testing various business plans, strategic policies and so on. Because such a forecast will be not used for budgetary allocation and control, its format and content can be arranged in any way to suit the purpose.

Nevertheless, a purpose-built budget forecast can also be used for 'What-if' analysis. We have already carried out quite a bit for Widget Makers Ltd – what if sales growth increased dramatically, what if capital expenditure was deferred, or brought forward – and so on.

The most important thing to remember in 'What-if'ing' is that it will only generate realistic predictions if all of the significant factors that impact on it are built into the model. For instance, if an item of expense that is significantly dependent upon sales volumes isn't in fact linked to them, then clearly the wrong answer will be obtained when the volumes are changed.

> The danger lies in building a model for a very specific purpose in which, for the sake of simplicity, no unnecessary relationships and links have been included, but later on using the model for a different purpose in which those links are essential.

But, if sales volumes are not going to be altered in a 'What-if' scenario, then no linking to them at all is needed.

The danger lies in building a model for a very specific purpose in which, for the sake of simplicity, no unnecessary relationships and links have been included, but later on using the model for a different purpose in which those links are essential.

## Summary

In this chapter:

- the effect of the time relationships between Sales, Variable Direct Cost cash payments, and Cash In from sales on cash flow was illustrated;
- it was shown that for Widget Makers Ltd a smooth growth to achieve increased sales, placed less burden on cash resources than a single sales peak;
- the timing of cash payments and receipts was seen to be a most significant factor of cash flow quality;
- reverse cash flow was explained, and illustrated in Widget Makers Ltd with a 50 per cent month-on-month sales growth;
- the principles of 'What-if' analysis were outlined.

# PART 5

■ ■ ■

# Handling VAT

Value Added Tax (VAT) is something that all but the smallest businesses must be concerned with. However, it may not be necessary for every budget controller and forecaster to take account of it, especially in departmental budgets.

As a rule of thumb:

- if the forecast is at the highest level of the business, *and* if it includes a cash flow forecast that is intended to represent the reality of cash movements, then accounting for VAT is essential;

- if a cash flow forecast that exists at any level in the business is intended to be a notional representation of cash movements only (see Chapter 9 'Reviewing the forecast – cash flow'), then accounting for VAT is unnecessary.

VAT can only be dealt with if there is a cash flow forecast and a budget forecast. Thus if a budget model does not have a cash flow forecast, VAT can be ignored entirely.

---

**Important:** Whilst the concept of VAT and the way in which it is handled in a cash flow forecast are simple and straightforward matters, the detailed rules applied by HM Customs and Excise are many, and in some instances very complex. Interpretation and application of the rules is, therefore, best done with the assistance of a qualified professional in liaison with HM Customs and Excise.

---

The VAT for a quarter is based on either *invoices* or *cash transactions*. Most businesses must base their return on invoices, but some may apply for it to be related to cash movements.

# 11

. . .

# VAT in the forecast

What is VAT? ■   213

Calculating and paying VAT ■

Budget and cash flow forecast VAT calculations ■

# What is VAT?

■ ■ ■

VAT is a tax, administered by HM Customs and Excise, that every business with a turnover greater than a disqualifying minimum, must add on to the selling price of its products or services. A business with a turnover greater than the disqualifying minimum *must* be registered for VAT with HM Customs and Excise, businesses with a lower turnover may apply for voluntary registration. A business not registered for VAT *must not* add the tax to their charges.

At intervals, usually quarterly, the VAT charged to customers is sent on to HM Customs and Excise. This payment, and the form associated with it, are known as the VAT return.

Businesses that are registered for VAT pay the tax on their own purchases, but reclaim it from HM Customs and Excise. The reclamation is not a separate process, but part of the VAT return. On the return form, the amount being reclaimed is subtracted from the amount due from sales, and the balance then sent to HM Customs and Excise. If the amount claimed is greater than the amount due from sales, the return is still made and the difference is then refunded to the business by HM Customs and Excise – see Figure 11.1 (below).

214

**Figure 11.1 The VAT return**

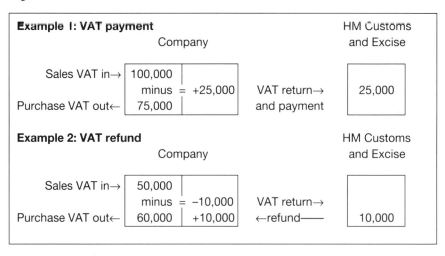

# Calculating and paying VAT

■ ■ ■

The VAT for a quarter is based on either invoices or cash transactions. Most businesses must base their return on invoices, but some may apply for it to be related to cash movements.

## Invoice accounting for VAT

To calculate VAT due to HM Customs and Excise, the VAT components of sales with an invoice date within the quarter are added up, then the VAT components of purchases with an invoice date within the quarter are added up and subtracted from the sales VAT sum.

The difference is then paid to (or refunded by) HM Customs and Excise.

## Cash accounting for VAT

To calculate VAT due to HM Customs and Excise, the VAT components of sales cash received within the quarter are added up, then the VAT component of cash paid out for purchases within the quarter are added up and subtracted from the sales VAT sum.

The difference is then paid to (or refunded by) HM Customs and Excise.

## VAT payment

The VAT return and payment fall due on the last day of the month following the quarter end. Thus if a VAT quarter is April to June, the last invoices or transactions included in the return for the period will occur on 30 June, and the return despatched to be received by HM Customs and Excise by 31 July.

> Errors and late payments, even one day, are liable to financial penalty.

Great care must be taken both in the completion of the VAT return, and in the timing of its despatch. Errors and late payments, even one day, are liable to financial penalty. On the other hand, sending the payment earlier than necessary can have a significant effect on cash flow if the quarter was profitable, as can sending it later than achievable if the quarter was not profitable.

Take a profitable quarter as in Example 1 (Figure 11.1). The £25,000 has been accumulating in the bank over the quarter, either offsetting borrowing charges, or earning interest. If the VAT return is completed, and despatched with the payment of £25,000 early in July, then nearly one month of its benefit to your bank account is lost. *But don't be late either* !

In an unprofitable quarter as in Example 2 (Figure 11.1), the £10,000 due as a refund has been lost from the bank over the quarter, and the sooner the return is despatched after 30 June the sooner the refund will be obtained and the sooner your bank account will benefit from it. *But don't rush it and create errors either* !

# Cash flow forecast calculations
■ ■ ■

This will be dealt with based on *VAT Invoice Accounting*, the cash accounting method will be outlined afterwards.

There are four stages to calculating VAT:

1  First, the amounts due on sales and purchase invoices are calculated in the budget forecast.
2  Secondly, the amount of VAT paid and received through the bank in the normal course of business is accounted for in the cash flow forecast.
3  Thirdly, the amount due to, or from, HM Customs and Excise each quarter is calculated in the budget forecast.
4  Fourthly, the amount paid to, or received from, HM Customs and Excise is accounted for in the cash flow forecast.

Not all purchases and sales are subject to VAT. In this example there are some purchases not subject to VAT, rent and business rates for instance, but the assumption is made that *all* sales are subject to VAT.

In schematic form, this is what the spreadsheet models need to do:

**Stages**

| Budget forecast | Cash flow forecast |
| --- | --- |
| (1) Calculate sales VAT due | VAT Cash In (2) |
| (1) Calculate purchase VAT due | VAT Cash Out (2) |
| (3) Calculate VAT return ——— link ——▶ | VAT return (4) |

We'll start by putting the calculations for stages (1) and (3) into the budget forecast.

> ★ The VAT calculations are already included on the illustration disc budget and cash flow models (P suffix).

# Budget forecast VAT

There is a convenient block of rows spare in the budget forecast, 96–111 just below the profit calculations.

Enter the row headings and formulae shown in Figure 11.2 (below). Note that only formulae for columns B and E are shown.

### Figure 11.2 (★BUDG01)  Budget forecast VAT calculations

```
      |         A        ||        B        ||            E              |
96         Enter VAT rate (%) >> 17.5
97
98    Expenses subject to VAT    B68-(B40+B48+B57+B58+B59)  E68-(E40+E48+E57+E58+E59)
99    --------------------------------------------------------------------------------
100   VAT due on purchases       B98*$VATRATE/100    E98*$VATRATE/100
101
102   VAT due from sales         B15*$VATRATE/100    E15*$VATRATE/100
103   --------------------------------------------------------------------------------
104   Net VAT / month            B102-B100           E102-E100
105   --------------------------------------------------------------------------------
106   VAT return to Customs & Excise E106            SUM(B102:D102)-SUM(B100:D100)
107   --------------------------------------------------------------------------------
```

217

## Notes to Figure 11.2

1  Cell B96 provides the facility to enter the VAT rate, so that it can be easily changed if the rate alters. I have given B96 the name VATRATE.

2  The expenses subject to VAT are most easily calculated by subtracting from the total cost (row 68) all expenses that are not subject to VAT, which are:

> Wages (Temporary staff)
> Salaries (Widget production)
> Postage
> Rates
> Salaries

3  VAT due on purchases, and from sales, are calculated by multiplying them by the VAT rate (and dividing by 100). Note the $ prefix to VATRATE in the formulae to fix it for copying purposes.

4  Net VAT/month is sales VAT less expenses VAT.

5  Using VAT quarter periods of:

> Jan – Mar
> Apr – Jun
> Jul – Sep
> Oct – Dec

**Figure 11.3 (★BUDG01) VAT calculated in the budget forecast**

| | A | B | C | D | E | F | G | H | I | J | K | L | M | N |
|---|---|---|---|---|---|---|---|---|---|---|---|---|---|---|
| 96 | | | | | | | | | | | | | | |
| 97 | Enter VAT rate (%) >> | 17.5 | | | | | | | | | | | | |
| 98 | Expenses subject to VAT | 48585 | 49410 | 99485 | 58585 | 58910 | 51285 | 50585 | 51410 | 50785 | 75585 | 51410 | 51285 | 697320 |
| 99 | | | | | | | | | | | | | | |
| 100 | VAT due on purchases | 8502 | 8647 | 17410 | 10252 | 10309 | 8975 | 8852 | 8997 | 8887 | 13227 | 8997 | 8975 | 122031 |
| 101 | | | | | | | | | | | | | | |
| 102 | VAT due from sales | 16625 | 16625 | 16625 | 16625 | 16625 | 16625 | 16625 | 16625 | 16625 | 16625 | 16625 | 16625 | 199500 |
| 103 | | | | | | | | | | | | | | |
| 104 | Net VAT / month | 8123 | 7978 | -785 | 6373 | 6316 | 7650 | 7773 | 7628 | 7738 | 3398 | 7628 | 7650 | |
| 105 | | | | | | | | | | | | | | |
| 106 | VAT return to Customs & Excise | | | 15316 | | | | 20339 | | | 23139 | | | |
| 107 | | | | | | | | | | | | | | |

the VAT return is due in the month following the end of each period – April, July, October and January of the following year. The formulae shown for April (column E) subtract the VAT due on purchases from the VAT due from sales in January to March. Replicate the formulae for July and October. Because we do not have a forecast for the previous year, a dummy VAT return figure has been entered in January by picking up the figure from the next return in April (E106).

Figure 11.3 (opposite) shows the VAT calculations for the whole year, note that the Net VAT/month for March is negative, because the VAT on purchases is greater than for sales in that month.

## Cash flow forecast VAT

Now the calculations for stages (2) and (4) in the cash flow forecast.

There is a convenient block of rows spare in the cash flow forecast, 70–80 just below the key indicators.

Enter the row headings and formulae shown in Figure 11.4.

### Figure 11.4 (∗CASH01) Cash flow forecast VAT calculations

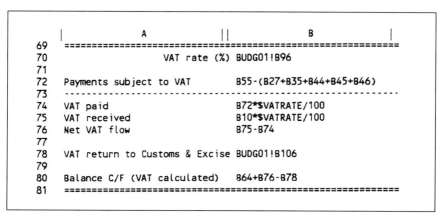

```
              |            A          ||             B              |
69  =============================================================
70                      VAT rate (%) BUDGO1!B96
71
72  Payments subject to VAT       B55-(B27+B35+B44+B45+B46)
73  - - - - - - - - - - - - - - - - - - - - - - - - - - - - - - - -
74  VAT paid                      B72*$VATRATE/100
75  VAT received                  B10*$VATRATE/100
76  Net VAT flow                  B75-B74
77
78  VAT return to Customs & Excise BUDGO1!B106
79
80  Balance C/F (VAT calculated)  B64+B76-B78
81  =============================================================
```

## Notes to Figure 11.4

1  Cell B70 picks up the VAT rate from the budget forecast. Again I have given this cell (B70) the name VATRATE.

Figure 11.5 (★CASH01) VAT calculated in the cash flow forecast

| | A | B | C | D | E | F | G | H | I | J | K | L | M | N |
|---|---|---|---|---|---|---|---|---|---|---|---|---|---|---|
| 69 | | | | | | | | | | | | | | |
| 70 | | | | | | | | | | | | | | |
| 71 | VAT rate (%) 17.5 | | | | | | | | | | | | | |
| 72 | Payments subject to VAT | 48585 | 49410 | 99485 | 58585 | 58910 | 51285 | 50585 | 51410 | 50785 | 75585 | 51410 | 51285 | 697320 |
| 73 | | | | | | | | | | | | | | |
| 74 | VAT paid | 8502 | 8647 | 17410 | 10252 | 10309 | 8975 | 8852 | 8997 | 8887 | 13227 | 8997 | 8975 | 122031 |
| 75 | VAT received | 16625 | 16625 | 16625 | 16625 | 16625 | 16625 | 16625 | 16625 | 16625 | 16625 | 16625 | 16625 | 199500 |
| 76 | Net VAT flow | 8123 | 7978 | -785 | 6373 | 6316 | 7650 | 7773 | 7628 | 7738 | 3398 | 7628 | 7650 | 77469 |
| 77 | | | | | | | | | | | | | | |
| 78 | VAT return to Customs & Excise | 15316 | 0 | 0 | 15316 | 0 | 0 | 20339 | 0 | 0 | 23139 | 0 | 0 | 0 |
| 79 | | | | | | | | | | | | | | |
| 80 | Balance C/F (VAT calculated) | 32432 | 51603 | -3235 | -16768 | -7209 | -3950 | -21541 | 453 | 2988 | -46866 | -17697 | -15750 | 77469 |
| 81 | | | | | | | | | | | | | | |

2   The payments subject to VAT are most easily calculated by subtracting from the total cash out (row 55) all cash out not subject to VAT, which are:

> Wages (Temporary staff)
> Salaries (Widget production)
> Postage
> Rates
> Salaries

3   VAT paid and received, are calculated by multiplying them by the VAT rate (and dividing by 100). Note the $ prefix to VATRATE in the formulae to fix it for copying purposes.
4   Net VAT flow is VAT received less VAT paid.
5   VAT return to HM Customs & Excise is picked up from the budget forecast.
6   Balance C/F (VAT calculated) adds the VAT flow and subtracts the VAT return.

Figure 11.5 (opposite) shows the VAT flow and resulting bank balance for the year.

## Closing balances compared

Now that VAT calculations have been added, the resulting balance carried forward will usually be higher than before in non VAT return months. This is because although the VAT paid out on purchases (an average of £10,169/month) has been taken from the cash flow, this is more than offset on a monthly basis by the VAT received (an average of £16,625/month). In VAT return months though, when the VAT due to HM Customs and Excise is paid, it will usually be lower.

Figure 11.6 (page 222) shows the original Balance C/F together with version that includes the VAT flow.

And that completes the calculations for VAT invoice accounting.

## VAT cash accounting

The principles of constructing VAT calculations under the cash accounting scheme are almost the same as for the invoice scheme. There is only one difference, the VAT return to HM Customs and Excise is not based on the invoice values in the budget, but on the cash paid and received in the cash flow.

So, to convert what has already been built into a cash accounting version:

**Figure 11.6 (✶CASH01 – Chart 3)**
**Original and VAT included balances C/F**

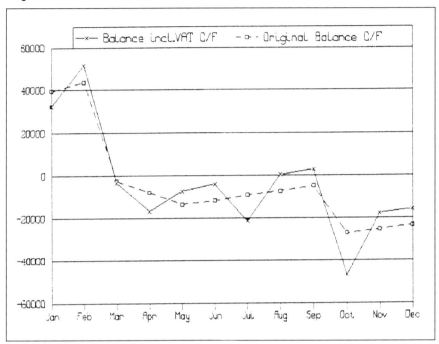

1   In the budget forecast, delete the row (106) that calculates the VAT return.

2   In the cash flow forecast, in row (78) headed 'VAT return to Customs & Excise', replace the links to the budget forecast with formulae in the VAT payment months (April, July, October – and January from the previous year) that sum the Net VAT flow for the previous three months. Thus in April (column E) enter:

**SUM(B76:D76)**

And that's that!


## Monitoring and reviewing

The methods already described for monitoring and reviewing are the same with or without VAT calculations, but remember that only actuals entered in the budget forecast will be picked up for the VAT return calculation. In other words, the rule about putting actuals into the lowest point in the dependency hierarchy still apply.

# Summary

In this chapter:

- the concept of Value Added Tax (VAT) was explained;
- it was shown that VAT calculations *must* be included if the cash flow forecast is intended to present a realistic view of the company's bank account;
- the principle of the quarterly VAT return was examined, and the importance of its timing for cash flow demonstrated;
- VAT calculations for invoice accounting were added to the budget and cash flow forecasts;
- it was seen that accounting for VAT usually means a gradually improving bank balance between VAT returns, as compared with the balance when VAT is not accounted for;
- the minor modifications necessary to convert the models to VAT cash accounting were detailed.

223

# Appendix 1
# Computer and spreadsheet glossary
■ ■ ■

*This glossary covers all of the computer and spreadsheet terms used in the book. Where the topic is more fully covered elsewhere a reference to it is also provided.*

**Address**   In a spreadsheet, a cell location described by the Column and Row that it occupies.

**Bit**   Binary Digit, one element of a Byte.

**Byte**   8 or 16 or 32 Bits, the smallest unit of computer data.

**Disc**   An instruction storage device.

**DOS**   (Disc) Operating System, the software which enables instructions to be easily given to the computer.

**Cell address**   See Address.

**Cell reference**   A special form of cell address (Chapter 4, Non-essential but useful techniques)

**File**   A set of instructions grouped together, for example, a word processed document or a set of data.

**File name**   The identifying name of a file.

**Floppy disc**   A transportable instruction storage device.

**Function**   In a spreadsheet, ready made instructions for a wide variety of uses. (Chapter 3, Principal facilities ... etc, Functions)

**Hard disc**   A (usually) fixed internal high capacity instruction storage device.

**Hardware**   The visible parts of a computer, eg processor, keyboard, VDU and printer, and the physical components inside them.

**Keyboard**   Enables instructions to be given to the computer.

**Kilobyte**   1024 (say 1000) Bytes

**Linking (File)**   Referring to a cell address in a different spreadsheet file. (Chapter 3, Multi-sheet and three-dimensional spreadsheets)

**Linking (Sheet)**   Referring to a cell address on another sheet of the spreadsheet. (Chapter 3, Multi-sheet and three-dimensional spreadsheets)

**Linking (Spreadsheet)**  Referring to a cell address elsewhere on the same spreadsheet. (Chapter 3, Principal facilities ... etc)

**Macro**  A sequence of instructions that are carried out automatically from a single command. (Chapter 3, Principal facilities ... etc, Macros)

**Megabyte**  1000 Kilobytes

**Memory**  A temporary store within the computer, into which instructions are copied from a disc. (Chapter 4, Essential practices and conventions, regular saving)

**MS-DOS**  A (Disc) Operating System manufactured by (M)icro(S)oft in very common use throughout the world.

**Named range**  In a spreadsheet, giving a *Range* a name, for example 'FRED'. (Chapter 3, Principal facilities ... etc, Naming Ranges)

**Processor**  The Integrated Circuit (chip) which is the heart of a computer.

**Range**  In a spreadsheet, a single expression of more than one cell address. See also Named range. (Chapter 3, Principal facilities ... etc, Ranges)

**Software**  The instructions that drive the hardware.

**VDU**  Visual Display Unit (Screen).

225

# Appendix 2
# Budgeting and forecasting glossary

■ ■ ■

*This glossary covers all of the budget and forecasting terms used in the book. Where the topic is dealt with more fully elsewhere, a reference to it is also provided.*

**Asset**   An item of realisable value. (Chapter 5, Cost Categories ... etc)

**Budget**   Used by itself the term usually refers to *Budget Allocation*. (Chapter 1)

**Budget allocation**   Financial limits allocated to *Expense* and *Revenue* headings, often calendarised. (Chapter 1)

**Budget forecast**   Expected *Revenue* and *Expense* for a budgeting period, based on rationale considerations and experience. (Chapter 1)

**Capital expenditure (expense/cost)**   Expenditure on items that possess a realisable value. See also Asset. (Chapter 5, Cost Categories ... etc)

**Cash in**   The cash received for *Revenue* earned. Also known as Income in the UK. (Chapter 1)

**Cash out**   The cash paid out for *Costs* (or expenses) incurred. (Chapter 1)

**Constant direct cost**   Costs associated directly with the product, but not significantly affected by product volumes. (Chapter 5, Cost Categories ... etc)

**Cost**   Incurred *Expense*, not necessarily yet paid for by *Cash Out*. (Chapter 1)

**Credit (Days/weeks etc)**   In forecasting, the period of time between *Cost* and *Cash Out*, or between *Revenue* and *Cash In* (Chapter 1)

**Creditor**   The one *to* whom money is owed. See also debtor.

**Debtor**   The one *from* whom money is due. See also creditor.

**Depreciation**   The amount by which the value of a *fixed asset* reduces. (Chapter 1, Profit and Loss Forecasts)

**Direct cost**   Any cost directly associated with the product. See also Constant direct and Variable direct. (Chapter 5, Cost Categories ... etc)

**Expense (expenditure/cost)**   See Cost (Chapter 1)

**Fixed asset**   An item of realisable value. (Chapter 5, Cost Categories ... etc)

**Gross profit**   Profit after *direct costs* are deducted from the *revenue*. (Chapter 1)

**Income**   See Cash In.

**Indirect (cost)**   Another word for *overheads*. (Chapter 5, Cost Categories ... etc)

**Loss**   A negative value of *profit* (Chapter 1)

**Net profit**   Profit after *overheads* are deducted from *gross profit*. (Chapter 1)

**Overhead (cost)**   Costs not directly associated with the (or a specific) product. (Chapter 5, Cost Categories ... etc)

**Period**   The time interval between successive forecasting elements – usually one calendar month or four weeks. (Chapter 5, The forecasts duration ... etc)

**Profit**   A loose term, most often used instead of *net profit* (Chapter 1)

**Revenue**   The value of *income* earned, but not necessarily received. See Cash in (Chapter 1)

**Span**   The time span of a budget (or other) forecast. Usually one year. (Chapter 5, The forecasts duration ... etc)

227

**Variable direct cost**   Cost directly associated with the product, and which vary significantly according to product volumes. (Chapter 5, Cost Categories ... etc)

**'What-if'**   A general term for the testing of possible circumstances, strategic proposals and the like. (Chapter 10)

# Index

■ ■ ■

absolute addresses and copying them
36
accruals 196
automatic recalculation
care in use 55
averages
different ways of calculating 72

backing up
essential practice 51
budget
definition 4
deciding the requirements 80
single or departmental 80
budget allocation 172
budget forecast
definition 4
example using a spreadsheet 63
expense assumptions 120
summary of entries 129
budgeting process 5, 78
budgets
number of periods 94
budgets and forecasts
for budget management 16
for planning and what if 17
for cost control 18
for raising finance 18
for cash flow control 20

capital cost category
definition 82
cash flow
impacts on 9
example of a firework
manufacturer 9
example of a supermarket 10
cash flow forecast
definition 7
example using a spreadsheet 67

cash flow offsets in the example 113
categorising cost headings 91
cause and effect – where to start 147
check sum
concept and example 54
for the example cashflow 111
for example budget 102
in the budget 111
column width 31
constant direct cost category
definition 86
copying cell contents 31
copying functions 34
cost categories
general definition 82
definition of capital 83
definition of start up 84
definition of variable direct 85
definition of constant direct 86
definition of overheads 87
cost headings
general considerations 88
choosing for the example budget
91
used by Widget Makers Ltd 91
cumulative totals
ways of calculating 72
cursor – and moving around 30

date and time stamping
essential practice 52
example of use 57

earlier and later sales receipts
impact on cash flow 204
entering numbers and text 30
essential practices
general 50
file naming
example of use 57

fixed (locked) column and row
    headings 70
flat sales profile
    impact on cash flow 201
forecast duration
    considerations 94
forecasts
    not the sole province of accountants
    11
formatting the presentation 40
functions 32

graphs (charts)
    examples 42
gross profit
    of each product 166

illustration disc
    obtaining x
illustration disc
    use of in the book 26
inserting and deleting rows and
    columns 37

just in time 20

key ratios 134

linking 46
    the budget to the sales forecast 100
    the cash flow to the sales forecast
    and budget 107

macros and an example 46
memory
    RAM 51
multi-sheet spreadsheets 46

named ranges 44
nominal ledger
    alignment with cost headings 89
numbers of rows and columns 30

overhead cost category
    definition 87

performance monitoring
    principles 173
    comparing actual with allocated 176
    setting up in the examples 180
percentages
    uses 72
performance monitoring
    frequency 174

the source of actual figures 174
recording actual figures 185
reviewing after actual data entered
    188

periods
    used in budgets 94
principal facilities and functions 28
profit & loss forecast
    definition 6
protecting cells
    essential practice 53

RAM (Random Access Memory) 51
ranges 44
rapid sales growth
    impact on cash flow 207
reiteration process 140
revenue (income) headings
    used by Widget Makers Ltd 93
reverse cash flow 207

SUM function introduced 34
sales forecast
    example using a spreadsheet 56
sales volume assumptions 118
sales volume peaks
    impact on cash flow 201
save copies of the example 98
saving
    essential practice 50
simple cause and effect 142
    improving gross profit 149
    trial and error 154
    increased overheads 158
    single large expenses, capital and
        start-up 160
    increased constant direct costs 160
    timing changes 162
    all change! 165
    a summary 148

smooth sales growth
    impact of cash flow 202
spreadsheets – what they are 27
start up cost category
    definition 84
structure
    of the book ix
three-dimensional spreadsheets 46
time and date stamping
    essential practice 52
titles and windows 70

VAT
    calculating 215
    cash flow forecast 219
    impact on cash flow 221
    what it is 214

variable direct cost category
    definition 85
version numbering
    essential practice 52
'what if' analysis 208